WITHOUT YOU

LIVING WITH LOSS

WITHOUT YOU

LIVING WITH LOSS

COMPILED AND EDITED BY
ORLAITH CARMODY

**All proceeds from the
sale of this book go to**

Our
Lady's
**Hospice
& Care**
Services

Harold's Cross
& Blackrock
Respite Rehabilitation Reassurance

Ballpoint Press

Published in 2018 by Ballpoint Press
4 Wyndham Park, Bray,
Co Wicklow, Republic of Ireland.

Telephone: 00353 86 821 7631
Email: ballpointpress1@gmail.com
Web: www.ballpointpress.ie

ISBN 978-0-9954793-9-5

While every effort has been made to ensure the accuracy
of all information contained in this book, neither the author nor
the publisher accepts liability for any errors or omissions made.

Book design and production by Joe Coyle Media&Design,
joecoyledesign@gmail.com

Cover Design by Alan Hatton

All photographs from writers' personal collections

Printed and bound by GraphyCems

For Kieran

Contents

Talking about the death of loved ones, gives us the strength to live with loss.

In the darkest moments of grief, we can all benefit from the light that comes from sharing our suffering with others.

I hope this book reminds people they are never alone, and that there is always hope for the future.

Leo Varadkar TD
An Taoiseach

Oifig an Taoisigh, Tithe an Rialtais, Baile Átha Cliath 2, D02 R583, Éire.
Office of the Taoiseach, Government Buildings, Dublin 2, D02 R583, Ireland.

Introduction and Acknowledgements

OUR Lady's Hospice in Harold's Cross is a very special place. I'm sure Blackrock is equally so, but it is Harold's Cross that has personal meaning for me. I drove in for the first time in 1988, down a long avenue with fields on either side, now long built over as the campus has evolved into a centre of excellence. I was a young woman in my twenties, and very daunted by what I would find. But I was met by a kind, elderly nun and a very smart young nurse called Adrienne. They told me that they would find the perfect place there for my husband, because we were so young, and we would need our privacy. Their mission would be to mind me as much as to mind him for the time he had left and for as long as I needed it afterwards.

I felt the weight of three years of battling for him lift off my shoulders. They understood, and gave me the confidence to do the next big thing. I went back to St Vincent's private hospital, and found the way to tell Kieran that the time had come to move to hospice care. In the end, it was better than we ever thought it could be. Our days were made good by lots more of that understanding and kindness.

The work of the Hospice is only possible because of the support of thousands of people — those who are neighbours and friends, those who have loved people who have spent time there, and those who hear about the work and want to support it because it feels right. Whichever category you find yourself in, thanks for picking up this book.

Writing is a very powerful way of dealing with feelings, but even so, asking people to write a letter directly to someone they have loved and lost is not easy. Reactions are mixed. Some get the idea immediately and say: 'If it helps just one person, I'll do it'. Others quietly decline, saying their feelings are too personal, or too hard to capture, or too difficult to share. And that's okay too. Taking part in an endeavour such as this one is not for everyone.

To those who did take part, who contributed the extraordinary letters in this book, my huge appreciation. Your openness of spirit and willingness to delve into really personal moments, in the interest of helping others, is noble. You have put your hearts firmly on your sleeves, and shared with us intimate details of your lives and your loved ones, to our great benefit. We are honoured to know you.

The letters are all so brilliant and different; the approaches to grieving and loss as unique as the set of circumstances which lead to the loss. But they have one thing in common, an absolute understanding that we are better people for having known those who are gone. Our writers were willing to generously share their experience in the hope that it brings you some solace as you deepen your own understanding of parting. Whatever stage you are at, our wish is that you find comfort and peace.

Some very special thanks are due, firstly to the staff of Our Lady's Hospice. You are unsung heroes who make tough times bearable for so many people. A special shout out to Jeanne McDonagh — who from the outset believed in the idea — and to Carina O'Neill, Eleanor Flew and the team who organise the Light Up a Life event each year and other creative fundraisers. Your work keeps the whole show on the road.

To my own team at Gavin Duffy and Associates — Grainne Lynn, Jayann Maher, Geraldine O'Callaghan and Aldona Fabisiak. Thanks for always going one step beyond the call of duty! It is so much appreciated.

To DJ Simon Young and my brother-in-law Eamon Duffy thanks so much for making those calls, twisting those arms and opening those doors. You are world-class 'connectors' — people who put people in touch with other people for no personal gain, but simply because you can, and because it results in good things.

A big thank you to Alan Hatton for the cover design, publisher PJ Cunningham for the sounding board and clear direction, and to An Taoiseach, Leo Varadkar, for supporting the concept very early on.

Finally, to my husband of 25 years, Gavin Duffy, and my four beautiful young people — Lorcan, Cormac, Cathal and Aislinn — thanks for always being there for me. I couldn't do a thing without you.

Orlaith Carmody
April, 2018

Foreword

IN the past many works on bereavement and loss were written by experts, based on their work with distressed clients, leading to theories about stages of grief that felt dry and prescriptive. In contrast, this is a book of many voices, from all walks of life. It reveals how the experience of death and response to it, is as varied as the human condition. It is to be welcomed, read slowly, and perhaps dipped into in quiet moments when our hearts need to know that there is a place beyond the desolation of loss.

To love is to know joy and the vulnerability and fragility of life.

Grief pulls us into a small, internal, painful space, populated by frightening feelings. Yes there is sadness, loneliness and anger but also envy, shameful relief or the torment of trying to locate meaning in the loss too fast. The endless unanswered cry of: "Why did it happen to me, to him?"

We do not have to be diminished by grief if we greet it with surrender and awareness.

As we surrender to grief we give voice to it, in whatever form works for us — speaking to friends, writing, listening to music, walking — whatever holds us at this time. With awareness, which emerges in being listened to and listening with kindness to ourselves, gradually the pain diminishes.

The holding at times needs skilful means, courage and patience, the stillness of prayer or meditation, and sometimes a trained listener to manage our reactivity or support us facing areas or feelings that are too frightening.

One young man who had cared beautifully for his elderly mother, yet became very depressed upon her death, found the exercise of writing out the story of her last days a great relief. *"I was carrying the story in my mind, going over it again and again. I was afraid I would forget it and that would be a final abandoning of her. I wrote it down and now it is there. I was walking the other day and for the first time in a year my mind was clear."*

Gradually we become more spacious internally, able to be with love and loss, able to remember the other in all their strengths and weakness. More spacious with ourselves, allowing ourselves to discover who we are again in this new way of being. Moving forward with a deeper sense of the preciousness of all life, risking connecting again. That connection may come in small ways, glimpsing the setting sun from a train window, or the light in the eyes of a grandchild, and we are here again present and living.

Dr Ursula Bates
Principal Chartered Clinical Psychologist,
Our Lady's Hospice and Care Services

I was surrounded by Black Cabs and red buses. I had a constant hum of the tube as a companion. All of them seemed to sing a song of you. I visited any place I could remember we'd been and I felt you beside me.

Rob Morgan writes to Dermot Morgan

Dear Dermot

SO, yeah, I call you Dermot now.

Calling you 'Pops' when you were here was the most natural thing in the world, but since you've been gone it's felt less and less normal. It's just like how I no longer call myself Bobby; I started using Rob after you died. Maybe both would have changed anyway, as I grew up, but we didn't get the chance to find out, did we? You don't choose when you die, but for a man who made his career from great timing, you screwed the pooch on this one.

It's over twenty years now and the fact that I'm fighting a lump in my throat and tears are threatening to roll down my face at any minute suggests that I still miss you — a lot. It's better than it was and it gets better with every day that passes, but there is still a Dermot-shaped hole in my life. It's a much smaller hole than twenty years ago, though. Time really is a healer.

There are obvious things that come with bereavement and grief, such as the fact that the decedent is physically no longer in one's life. I felt that, but less than I thought. Weirdly, the fact that you and Mom separated, meant that I had dealt with the fact that you weren't physically in my life every day much sooner than I had any right to. It's funny the things that catch you out though. I hate, hate, HATE that we'll never have a picture of us together where I'm an adult. I'll forever be 17 (at best) in any pictures of us. The fact that you'll be forever 45 is no comfort.

I'm writing this on a flight to Paris, for work. I never took any career advice you offered. Like any kid, I wanted to find my own path, but that doesn't mean I wasn't listening. I know that you wanted me working with numbers and that you wished that I had done French in school. Well, guess what? I'm learning French for work and I'm a qualified accountant. I did study hotel management, as I always threatened to. I know it was something you weren't all that keen on, but the long hours weren't that long and the low pay wasn't that low. It also brought me closer to you, allowed me to go places where we had made memories.

In London, I lived in Victoria (I tried to get St. Margaret's or Fulham, but that didn't quite work out). I was surrounded by black cabs and red buses. I had a constant hum of the tube as a companion. All of them seemed to sing a song of you. I visited any place I could remember we'd been and I felt you beside me. It also nearly killed me, like it killed you — so I got the hell out.

Do you remember where we last hung out, just you and me? I didn't, until I found myself working there! By a twist of fate, the job I got in 2008, when I left London and came back to Dublin, was in The Merrion Hotel. Something about the place seemed so right to me, so warm and so familiar. Then it hit me — December 1997. The hotel had just opened and we had a chance for a last catch up before I went to Germany for Christmas. The Cellar Bar, the warm wood panelling, the stone walls; it was there that we had last hung out! What better place to start over. I spent six years there (during which I started retraining as an accountant); many of the guys I worked with had been working there since it opened — since we had been there. My memories of there have become a proxy for the memories we didn't get to make.

By now, I am a qualified accountant — something that I joke to people would be a source of great shame to you! I left hotels behind, but I still go back to The Merrion for a dose of our memories. I walk past the front of Guilbauld's and think that someday I'm going to bring Ruth there and show her where you went when Newshounds didn't get greenlit by RTÉ. Normal people suffer setbacks and hide, you went for a Michelin starred lunch. F*** the begrudgers!

I go to Doheny's where a picture of you and Don hangs in the back bar. I go to The Troc (once in a blue moon) to see your picture there too. Anywhere that we have shared memories of, I go. I'm lucky that I can do that and I feel guilty for that, others don't get so lucky. It's the only thing I can say to people who are grieving, find somewhere you enjoyed time with the person who left you and be with them there. It's how I get through the tough patches; the patches that come calling when the big life events roll around.

Life events, yeah... I'm still pissed at you about those: my leaving cert, my 21st, my college graduation, leaving for the UK, coming home, marrying Ruth! You were meant to be there for those, I hate you not being there and I also hate you for not being there! Don has kids now (his eldest is named after you), Ben has moved to Canada — you should have been here. That's probably the hardest thing, because I can't do anything about that feeling. If I'm ever asked about grieving, it's the one area I don't have an answer for. I don't know how to make it feel any better.

That's the kicker with death. You can't figure it all out, but we never think like that. We always think that it will eventually be behind us, that it will eventually stop hurting. I'm starting to believe that it doesn't. I'm starting to think that that pain is actually your way of letting me know you'll always be there. Now, instead of looking forward to the day when it'll stop hurting, I embrace that there'll always be part of you with me. If it ever really stopped hurting, if that hole was ever fully closed, that would mean that I've stopped missing you. I'd never want that. Anyway, enough of my bar stool psychology — if my theory was right, someone else would have had it by now.

There's so much more that I want to tell you, but the fasten seatbelt light has just come on again and the cabin crew are asking us to put our laptops away, so I'm thinking that's what I should do (you and Mom did teach us to respect authority figures after all). It would have been easier to tell you my feelings in person, rather than putting them in this letter, but I suppose we can't always get what we want. Just know this, you were a fantastic Dad — something I'll always remember, regardless of how long you've been gone, I just would have liked a few more decades of you.

Love you,
Rob

ROB MORGAN

Born in 1980, I'm the second of Dermot's three sons. Don (the eldest) and Ben (the youngest) have their own experience of his loss and, as is normal, no two grieving processes are ever the same.

I was 17 when Dermot died suddenly, in the middle of my Leaving Cert mock exams — not an

easy set of circumstances. I did what I think Dermot would've wanted, knuckled down and got through the exams, processing his loss at the same time. I studied Hospitality Management at Dublin Institute of Technology and had a very enjoyable first career in hotel management. In 2016, I successfully completed my retraining as an accountant and now work with an aircraft maintenance company in Dublin.

I never had any interest in following in Dermot's footsteps, but for a few years I threw on his sparkly jacket and stepped on stage to judge the "Lovely Girls Competition" at Ted Fest on Inis Mór and at similar events in Dublin. At one such Dublin event, on a filthy autumn evening, I met my now wife, Ruth. We were married in July 2017 and even though Dermot wasn't there on the day, it's hard not to think that he played his part in turning fate to bring us together.

I tell them about you collecting money for the black babies when you were at school. And you told me you used to rob the box, because you were a black baby. I hope you are not annoyed with me!

Philomena Lynott writes to Phil Lynott

Dear Philip

I HAVE started to write to you many times before, but my tears just keep dropping on the page and smudging it. I have so much to tell you, I wish I could phone you. I do miss hearing your voice. You know I love you with all my heart. No one will ever know how much you meant to me. I had thought that your death was a waste, and a destruction. I'm only beginning to learn that your life was a gift.

My whole life changed after you passed on. I was numb. I couldn't cope. I just shut down. I could not listen to music, I just wanted to follow you, and be with you to comfort you. Then the postman started bringing me letters from all around the world, from fans who were heartbroken at losing you. I have kept all the letters and answered them all by hand. They told me how your music inspires them. Some of them had met you and you were very kind to them, so they decided they wanted to commemorate you, and they started sending me money to build a statue. They kept me alive and busy. They became my friends. They come to visit your resting place and then they visit me and have a cup of tea.

And we talk about you. I tell them about you collecting money for the black babies when you were at school. And you told me you used to rob the box, because you were a black baby. I hope you are not annoyed with me! Some of your fans have their babies called after you. I get invited to rock shows because I'm your Ma. I get treated very well.

I have noticed in the last few years a lot of your buddies have gone to stay with you. So I don't worry about you as much as I did. I can imagine you all having a rock concert in heaven. I still visit schools and prisons telling the youngsters about the danger of drugs. If I can stop another mother or father going through the pain of losing their young ones.

I hope you are looking after Granny Sarah. Give her a big hug for me. I have to go now because I'm starting to cry and be sad. It will not be long before I can see you, and give you a big kick in the bum for breaking my heart.

Hugs and xxx for ever.

From your Ma

Philomena Lynott

PHILOMENA LYNOTT

Philomena "Phyllis" Lynott is an Irish author and entrepreneur. She is the mother of Thin Lizzy frontman Phil Lynott, and her autobiography, *My Boy*, documents the relationship between her and her son, who died in 1986. She was the proprietor of the Clifton Grange Hotel, Manchester, which provided accommodation for a number of bands in the 1970s including Thin Lizzy.

Philomena's home "White Horses" in Sutton, Dublin is a shrine to Phil and she regularly hosts fans from all over the world to tea and chat.

I miss talking to you every day, you were the girl I loved talking to most in the world. The heartache of losing you will never be healed, but you have left us with millions of exquisite thoughts and memories.

Gloria Hunniford writes to Caron Keating

Dear Caron

WHAT a joy and privilege for over 41 years to have you as my most precious and loving daughter.

I feel so proud to be your Mum and I could not have wished for a more glorious daughter; spirited, caring, loving and full of fun.

You showered endless love and joy on our lives and brought light and rainbows to us daily. Although our relationship has always been exceptionally deep, during the last seven years there have been constant new depths and discovery, but through all your pain and suffering, you have brought such warmth, love, laughter and friendship.

Watching you bravely battle with cancer has taught me so much about positivity, tenacity, dignity, spiritual growth and integrity. You are a total inspiration, not only to your family, but to all those lives you have touched.

You and Russ have given us the precious and ultimate gift in two beautiful boys, Charlie and Gabriel, and you will live on through them. They will be a daily reminder of your spirit and individuality and all the values that you have taught them. Alongside Russ, Paul, Sandy, Michael and Stephen I will forever love and look after your cherished boys, as you would wish.

I miss talking to you every day, you were the girl I loved talking to most in the world. The heartache of losing you will never be healed, but you have left us with millions of exquisite thoughts and memories.

In Australia you used to say that you could not wait to have a cup of tea out of your favourite cup, at the kitchen table in Sevenoaks and with your incredible instinct and typical Irish timing, you made it back. Perhaps out of the endless memories, a few of the more recent ones will always shine out. Four weeks in Switzerland when, in the middle of concentrating on your healing and treatment, you also managed to organise my birthday celebrations, the Easter egg painting competition and a blissful Mother's Day, just you and me. It was the first time in three years that we had spent Mother's Day together and what a glorious day we had in the Swiss Alps, scoffing apple strudel and chatting non-stop.

How I treasure your gift, which you managed to paint in Australia despite your pain and frustration; beautiful tulips in a country frame which you carefully inscribed with love and kisses and lovingly placed in your suitcase for our special day together, which was yet another example of your generosity of spirit, which you radiated in abundance. You always did believe in angels and now you are one of God's brightest and most beautiful, so fly freely, my darling Caron, in your release from pain and know that every second I will carry you in my heart.

With all my love forever,
Mum

GLORIA HUNNIFORD
Gloria Hunniford was born in Portadown, County Armagh, Northern Ireland. She is a broadcaster and producer, known for *Loose Women* (1999), *That's*

Showbusiness (1989) and *Sunday, Sunday* (1982). Her daughter was the late TV presenter Caron Keating. Following an early career as an actress and singer, Gloria became the first woman to host her own daily radio show on BBC Radio 2. She was awarded the OBE (Officer of the Order of the British Empire) in the 2017 Queen's Birthday Honours List for her serves to Cancer Charities through Breast Screening Services and Cancer Support in Kent, England. The Caron Keating foundation is a fund raising cancer support charity set up by Gloria and her sons Paul and Michael.

You couldn't play the game in any other way
Winning meant that much to you.

Charlie McGettigan writes to Shane McGettigan

I'd get excited

I can still hear your key as it opened the door,
I loved those Friday nights.
And you'd laugh at your mother when she'd say "How much
more dirty stuff is in your bag?"

And I remember the way you'd gobble your food
And tell us how college was
And your sisters complained, "How can he be so rude?"
And you'd say "What's all the fuss?"

I'd get excited, just to look in your eyes.
I'd feel a flutter inside.
I'd get excited just to see you walk by
I couldn't hide my pride.

You'd play the piano before a big game,
With those big broken hands.
You'd play "Moonlight Sonata" It was always the same
And in the other room we'd dance.

I'd get excited, just to look in your eyes.
I'd feel a flutter inside.
I'd get excited just to see you walk by
I couldn't hide my pride.

And there were times I'd have to cover my face
With the reckless things that you would do.
You couldn't play the game in any other way
Winning meant that much to you.

And yet in winning you were quiet and mild
You couldn't face the light
When all around you were going crazy and wild
You'd keep it all inside.

I'd get excited, just to look in your eyes.
I'd feel a flutter inside.
I'd get excited just to see you walk by
I couldn't hide my pride.

Now though I feel sadness I also feel joy.
The memories we have
When I think of you now as a man as a boy,
They're only thoughts of love.

I'd get excited, just to look in your eyes.
I'd feel a flutter inside.
I'd get excited just to see you walk by
I couldn't hide my pride.

CHARLIE McGETTIGAN
**Charlie McGettigan is a singer songwriter from
Leitrim who has performed and written many
songs over a long and successful career. He won the
Eurovision Song Contest for Ireland in 1994 with**

the song, Rock n' Roll Kids, performed with Paul Harrington and written by Brendan Graham.

Charlie's 21-year-old student son Shane died in a construction accident in the USA in 1998, a few short weeks after arriving there to take up a summer job. Shane's friend Ronan Stewart was also killed in the accident.

Charlie wrote this song to commemorate Shane's life, and while it has been recorded, Charlie has never performed it in public.

I walked miles that afternoon on beautiful country roads with tears streaming down my face and the answers came to me – I was your mother and I would let you live your life however you were going to live it.

Marie Prior writes to Ciarán Prior

Dear Ciarán

I REMEMBER the rush of excitement and pure joy when I saw the words "pregnant" on the test. My life changed in that instant, my thoughts focusing on the fact that "we" would now mean three instead of two. It was a little after six in the morning and by the time I woke John with the news less than an hour later. I had already worked out that your birthday would be in January, which room in the house would become the nursery, and a million and one other ways that your arrival would impact our lives.

I tried to restrain my excitement as it was early days, but it was impossible. I was going to become a mother and you were going to flip my world on its head. We went to a family wedding that day and I can still remember your Dad putting a protective hand over my tummy that evening in a way that he had never done before. You were part of our own wedding two weeks after that and you made the day even more special because we were the only ones who knew you were about to become a new member of the family.

There were so many firsts over those weeks and months — seeing you at the first scan, hearing your heartbeat echo around the room that first time, telling the family and watching their excitement at the news and debating whether we should find out if you were a boy or a girl. In the end we decided to find out at the 25-week scan — but that was when our world came crashing down around us.

The obstetrician told us that you were a boy and almost within the same breath, that she was concerned about the development of your heart. We went from such a high to such a crash, it felt like my world had stopped turning. The week that followed while we waited to meet the pediatric cardiologist was one of the most surreal of my life. I could feel you moving and kicking and those kicks were so strong that I could not believe that there could be anything seriously wrong with your heart. We focused on the positives — you were growing well and all other developmental signs were good — so surely it was not going to be anything too serious.

We travelled to Dublin to see the cardiologist and she was the one who told us the extent of the very complicated heart defects that you had. We were in shock and trying to take it all in. This could not be right, this could not be happening. I remember asking her about the treatment options and she told us that it was not likely that they would be able to offer a treatment option. She told us that you would most likely die before you were born or immediately after and that we should consider a termination.

We left the hospital in a daze and that night I broke down in your Dad's arms and cried with such intensity that it scared me. I was your mother and you were my beautiful baby and I was being told that I had no way to save you.

The days that followed were a rollercoaster of emotions when I and your Dad tried to come to terms with what we had been told. I had always seen myself as a strong, independent, self-sufficient woman who was not prone to emotional outbursts, so this was new territory for me. Your Dad was my rock and despite his own emotional distress he protected me and loved me in a way I had never experienced before.

There were decisions to be made that were almost impossible to make. The Saturday after the diagnosis I went for a long walk and I spoke to you... I poured my heart out to you. I walked miles that afternoon on beautiful country roads with tears streaming down my face and the answers came to me — I was your mother and I would let you live your life how you were going to live it. I would do all I could to bring you into this world as healthy as possible and that meant getting back to normal, a new normal but normal.

We tried to enjoy the pregnancy as much as possible, although we never prepared the nursery at home. The hospital had told me not to bring in clothes or teddies for you, but I could not do that. I so clearly remember the day when I bought your vests and baby-gros and the most adorable little elephant teddy for you. I had to hide my tears before I brought them to the till that day, but I am glad now that I ignored what the hospital told me.

The night before you were born was one of the most difficult of my life. You were safe where you were, but as soon as you left my body you were on your own. Everything we were being told lead us to believe that you would not survive, or if you did, then it would be for seconds. I did not want to let you go, it was my job to keep you safe and there were many times that night that I thought about absconding from the hospital. But my reality was that I had to relinquish what little control I had, and let you do your own thing. Every mother faces this challenge eventually — mine just came much earlier than most.

And you certainly did your own thing, Ciarán. The decision for an emergency C-section was made approaching lunchtime on the Monday. As I was rushed to theatre they warned me that you most likely would not make a sound when you were born. But you roared your way into the world... and mine were not the only tears in the theatre that day. The resuscitation team were not required and it was decided that you were well enough for transfer to the ICU without any intubation. You were breathing on your own, against all the odds.

I was so proud of you that day — you were living your life in your own way. The pictures of your Dad holding you in the ICU within an hour of your birth are imprinted in my mind forever. Your wide open eyes, his face the picture of a proud Dad, no tubes and the most handsome baby in the world — all 8 lbs 15oz of you — the baby they told us would not thrive in the pregnancy!! Your Dad made the calls to pass on the joyful news that you had arrived and were doing well.

You were transferred to Crumlin Children's Hospital within hours of your birth — again living life your way — we had been told you would never make it to Crumlin. I was overjoyed and totally in love, and when your Dad brought me the pictures and the videos of you that night I felt as if I'd won the lotto.

I got to hold you the next day — my big, bouncing bright-eyed gorgeous little boy. We had your christening in the cardiac ICU in Crumlin and your grandparents and god-parents were there — another unexpected and treasured moment. You wore one of those lovely little baby-gros.

Your medical diagnosis remained the same, so how you were doing, what you were doing was unexplainable. You got out to a ward and your aunties and uncles got to meet you, but I could see that your efforts were taking their toll on you. I sat by your cot as much as I could and watched you — taking in everything about you — your dark hair, your long eyelashes, your sallow skin — to me you were the most handsome baby I had ever seen. Your name means "little dark prince" and it suited you to a tee.

The decision to operate was made the Thursday after you were born, with the operation planned for Friday the 13th. I remember asking the surgeon if they could operate on a different day, but they were so busy that they hadn't even realised the date.

That Friday started with an early phone call to let me know that my grandmother had passed away during the night, so my emotions were all over the place. Foremost in my mind was the thought that she had taken your place. You were called for surgery and the preps were done. The final minutes before you were to be transferred, we got to hold you in our arms with no leads, no monitors, as normally as possible, and we drank in every bit of you. Then you crashed right there in the room, literally as they arrived to take you for surgery.

We watched them resuscitate you. It was surreal... this could not be happening. When they rushed you to the ICU I collapsed on the chair and screamed. What came out was such a tortured sound, that of a wounded animal. Your Dad and the nurses tried to comfort me, to calm me, but the sobs and cries racked my body in an uncontrollable manner.

When we saw you in the ICU attached to tubes and monitors — it broke my heart. You looked like a different baby. You fought and fought, Ciarán, and that weekend was one of highs and lows. You rallied and you weakened and you rallied and you weakened. The medical team did everything they possibly could for you and when they told us on the Sunday that they were out of options we knew that your loss was inevitable. We were optimistic realists — we knew that you had a medical Everest to climb if you were going to survive, and there were so, so many times during your short life that I thought you were going to scale that mountain. But the cold harsh reality of life hit us square in the eyes that Sunday afternoon.

Holding you in our arms as you took your last breaths was physically one of the hardest things I have ever done. I have never known such pain... my heart broke... shattered into tiny pieces.

We brought you home that night... our neighbours and friends came and met you, it was like a dream. You slept between us that night and I never wanted the dawn to come. I wanted to stay like that forever with you sleeping peacefully between us.

I thought my granny died to take your place, but I know now that she went before you to be there to mind you when you left us, and that has given me such comfort in the darkest hours.

Closing that white coffin lid broke our hearts all over again... your little elephant teddy went with you. You looked adorable in the most beautiful outfit, bought for you by one of your Aunts.

The hours, weeks and months after your death were filled with tears, devastation, compassion, love, anger, pain and yet also with pride and joy. I was so proud of how you had lived your short life and I loved being able to talk about you in such detail, having had almost a week to love you and hold you and spend with you.

But the loneliness and the longing were intense. I was the mother with no baby... my body was still. Our house was too quiet. The stress and the trauma meant that I lost my pregnancy weight very quickly and this upset me even further. I had no baby and I did not even look like I had had a baby. It was devastating. There were so many firsts to deal with.

The first time I heard someone call a little boy by your name, he happened to be a dark-haired toddler with sallow skin, and time stood still. The first time I went to the supermarket and saw another mother with a baby of similar age buying nappies — I had never bought nappies. Our first wedding anniversary, the first Christmas without you, your first birthday, the first birth in our extended family after yours, my first day back at work... the list was endless.

There were times when I wondered how I would survive, how we would ever be happy again, and it was at those times that I felt an enormous responsibility to make you as proud of me as I had been and am of you. This was my motivation to continue. This was what got me out of bed on the days where I wanted to hide away from the world. This desire to make you proud got me showered and dressed and out of the house to face the world.

This pride drove me to fundraise in your memory and the organisation of that fundraiser kept me busy. A new mother with no baby needs to keep herself occupied.

I interviewed for a promotion at work within a few months of your birth while still on maternity leave. I almost bottled it, because the day beforehand I went into meltdown. It was your Dad's support, and that of good friends, in addition to fulfilling the desire to make you proud, that made me put on my uniform and put my best foot forward that morning.

That promotion at work lead me to have command of a State Ship the year after you were born. It was one of the proudest days of my career and one that I had worked hard to achieve, but it was tinged with sadness. I looked at the guests assembled on the quay wall on the day of the ceremony and the one that was missing was the bouncing toddler that should have been sitting on your Dad's knee.

Your sixth birthday falls this week — time has passed so quickly. Time has eased the pain of your loss but it is always there, we have learned how to live with it.

The arrival of your two little sisters in the past three years has definitely taken the edge off the devastation that we endured after we lost you. They are very aware of their big brother and your name is mentioned on a daily basis in the house. Our families have not forgotten you either.

I watch your sisters grow and develop their individual personalities and I wonder what you would have been like. The hardest part is that we will never know.

But what we do know is that you were a fighter who challenged the system and liked to take a shot at overcoming even the worst odds. You were courageous and lived life to the maximum. Your short life impacted on many and your story is one of hope. You have taught me that the worst of times and the darkest hours can be survived, and that love endures and makes us stronger than we believe possible.

You gave me the greatest gift Ciarán, you made me a mother; you showed me what unconditional love is. You gave me the courage to have more children, because that love is worth all the risks. You changed the relationship that

I have with your Dad and you made us stronger than we ever thought possible. You gave me the strength to survive and your life taught me that no one is an island... We may think we can do it on our own, but in truth we need to have those around us who will pick us up when we fall down.

You are always in my thoughts and in my heart,

With all my love,

Mam....xxx

MARIE PRIOR (GLEESON)

Marie Prior is a Lieutenant Commander in the Irish Navy. She has held a variety of appointments during her twenty year career including UN service with the 101st Infantry Battalion in Chad in 2009 and as the Officer Commanding of the LE AOIFE from 2013 to 2015. She currently works in the Personnel Management Section in Support Command Headquarters. She is married to John, a mechanical design engineer and they have three children. Their eldest son Ciarán was born with a complicated congenital heart defect and was six days old when he passed away in 2012. Their two younger daughters Laoise and Muireann live with them in the countryside in North Cork.

All in all, I cannot complain. Miss you every day but love being able to speak to you every day, without having you argue back!

Peter Casey writes to Patsy Casey

Dear Patsy

JUST checking in to give you an update. Well you always said: "He must have something special to achieve, or else he would be dead a long time ago!"

All the car crashes, getting shot, electrocuted and so on. I am still having them — the crashes — and would appreciate if you could use your influence to reduce them.

I still don't go to mass as often as you would like, and still cannot understand why they keep pushing the Rosary! You remember when I asked you why it was necessary to say the Hail Mary ten times, five times in a row. And you said, "If you were to tell me fifty times in a row, 'Mammy I love you', I would never get bored hearing it". To which I replied, "Just how insecure are you?" And you smacked me!

I still believe that once should be enough and twice is pushing it to the limits BUT 50 times, give me a break.

Anyway, back to the update. Your 38 grandchildren are all well, thanks I am sure to your intervention. My liver is still functioning at warp speed, defying all medical predictions, thanks again to your excellent gene pool.

You would be pleased and probably surprised at how religious your five grandchildren, that I was blessed with, have become. Certainly I can take no credit for that except that I suppose I paid the bills for the Catholic School that Helen insisted they go to!

I don't think however there will be any nuns or priests

in my five, as they are all actively dating. Having said that, since you left us, there have been numerous reports of many priests and nuns actively dating so you never know.

We have a new Pope called Francis who I think you would like. He seems very warm and open. We were at an audience with him and he is very sincere, but surprisingly quite chunky, I would say close to 265lbs. I like him except that he made John Paul 2 a saint quicker than you could do *The Times* crossword, and as you and I often argued, JP2 must have known what was going on.

As you know, I have lost a few of my closest friends this year and had a bad year physically so looking forward to 2018. Also as you know, I decided to bypass St Anthony when I lose things and just go directly to you. The logic behind this is that I would make promises to pay St Anthony, who by the way probably never existed, and certainly never got the money.

The great thing is that you have always delivered, and you don't charge, and I don't commit more sins by not paying up!

All in all, I cannot complain. Miss you every day but love being able to speak to you every day, without having you argue back!

I tell the children, if you have a problem, "Say a wee prayer to Patsy, it always works".

Thanks for looking after me and the rest of the clan.
Love you always and talk soon
Your favourite son
Peter

PS. Hope Leo is looking after you as well as he did on earth and tell him that unless he intervenes, fairly quickly in my golf game, driving in particular, he will not be getting many more prayers.

PPS. Tell Leo that he definitely needs to help/intervene personally with your other golfing son Hugh's chipping! If he does not, I think he may give up golf and become a Buddhist! In fairness to Leo, Hugh generally bypasses him and goes straight to the Son of the Boss when complaining!

PETER CASEY

Peter Casey is an entrepreneur who divides his time between Atlanta in the United States and his Irish home in Donegal. He is the founder and Executive Chairman of Claddagh Resources, a global recruitment and executive search business. He is best known as an investor on the RTÉ television programme *Dragons' Den*, in which he was one of the Dragons. He is the author of a book *The World's Greatest Company* about the Tata Group and contributes regularly to Irish newspapers.

I talk to you often, and some of you more than others. Mostly to ask for your help, but also to say thanks. I'm grateful, too, that your loss isn't still that sharp hurt, followed by that terrible ache. Time is giving in that.

Ethel Rohan writes to many people

Fires Inside

Dear Granny
I'm sorry I didn't want to kiss you in your coffin. You were my first dead body and I was scared.

Dear Helen
Before you died, Sister James took our class to the Mater Hospital to see you in your coma. I wanted us to sing to you because that can sometimes bring people back. But you had been trapped in that between place for years and many had already tried everything. Over three decades later and I still imagine us singing you back to life.

Dear Auntie Nora
You died in the hospital in the pink nightdress I bought you in Penneys with my pocket money. It was pretty. You were my favourite.

Dear Noelle
You were twenty-one and too beautiful in your coffin to be dead. I almost laughed out loud when I first saw you, thinking it was a joke, expecting you to sit up. Your family fixed the lipstick the undertaker painted on. All that night they kept saying how the first lipstick was wrong, how it wasn't you.

Dear Granny Mc

I'm sorry I fought with my parents and went out with friends the night you were buried. More, I'm sorry for the look on Daddy's face when I said my sitting in wasn't going to bring you back. I wanted to escape the feeling in our house—like things, Dad, were going to crack and break.

Dear Scoby

You told the joke so many times and everyone always fell for it:

"A fella back home died."

"Sorry to hear that. What did he die of?"

"He died of a Tuesday."

And so did you. A Tuesday in a long ago April. The Sunday night before your death, you and I screamed along with the jukebox to "Bat Out of Hell." Like the song, your accident landed you in the bottom of a pit. I placed a single yellow rose on your coffin, the colour of the burning sun.

Dear Amanda

I still see the stars tattooed on the inside of your wrist and hear the jangle of your bracelets. You loved to write and to read and to teach Annie Dillard. "How we spend our days is, of course, how we spend our lives." When I think I've nothing more to give, or that I can't do any better, I remember all you planned to do and how hard you would want to come back, and I press on.

Dear Mike

I flew five thousand miles and the undertaker lifted the lid off your coffin just for me. You were more brother than in-law. Alive, you could never have felt so cold. You were one of the brightest lights.

Dear Betty
All those summers, all those times with my two daughters. Back then, they were the youngest of your grandchildren. You and I sat on your kitchen floor, helping the girls build towers with wooden blocks. Laughing, they knocked the blocks down and together the four of us built them back up again. It's important, you showed us, falling and getting back up.

Dear Thomas
The last time I saw you, at that party, I avoided you. Depressed, suicidal, I was afraid you, dear friend, would look at me and know. Less than a week later, you took your own life. I had no idea. No one did. Imagine if we had talked that night and listened to the howl of each other's insides.

Dear Mammy
I'm sorry you suffered so much. Nothing I ever write will make up for the one story I can never tell: My mother lived well and full and happy. My three brothers, two sisters and I carried your coffin. People said they'd never seen the like. Dad said it made him proud. It was something we couldn't do for you in life, during your long struggle with mental illness, and then Alzheimer's. We lifted you. We raised you up.

Dear Mike Senior
My husband's father, you dropped dead in a field on your farm, looking out at all that you and God had made. A good death for a great man.

Dear Dad

You died three months after Mam. Four years later and that's still hard to take in. Mam's death was expected, yours was tragic and traumatic, from an operation gone wrong. You weren't ready to go. My brothers, sisters and I weren't ready to lose you.

We also carried your coffin, lowered you into the brown-black earth, and filled in your grave. I can still see you in your forever sleep, feel the weight of you on my right shoulder, and hear the dirt hit your coffin. It's all solace. Sacred. People said we gave you a fantastic send-off. Said it was so beautiful it hurt.

Years before, I rented a house in Wicklow — the garden county, your county. You and I walked the yellow-green fields and hills together, under the smile of the sun. All around us, the sway of tall trees, wheel of dark birds, and the wave of wild, colourful flowers.

You pointed out the pattern the trees made in the gaps, where their crowns didn't touch. I almost said something about loneliness and maybe the trees keep growing until they reach each other. But you weren't a man for such talk or feelings said out loud.

"Thank you," you said later, a slight tremble in your voice. "That was grand."

There's a part of me still there on that walk with you, the pair of us looking, marvelling.

Dear Declan

I didn't get to know you nearly well enough and yet I loved you. You were gentle, quiet, funny, and kind. I loved you most for how much you loved my sister. For how together you planned and hoped and dreamed. It still burns my eyes and throat that you were taken, and that some of my sister's fire went with you.

Dear All the Dead of my Heart
I talk to you often, and some of you more than others. Mostly to ask for your help, but also to say thanks. I'm grateful, too, that your loss isn't still that sharp hurt followed by that terrible ache. Time is giving in that.

I believe you're still with me. Why not? I feel you in the air around me, see you in the grace and goodness of others, hear you in the roar of the ocean, and sense you in the breeze at my back, ushering me forward.

It seems impossible that I ever wanted to die. My mind was so ill I lost the precious in each moment. Recovered, I now inhale the invisible wind, track the swell and crash of the white waves, hear the pulse of my veins in birdsong, laugh and love with family and friends, and rest in the sure, tender arms of the real and the imagined.

There are times I could kneel in wonder. Times I'm so happy it's almost too much. Times I feel each of you right here in my chest, flames that crackle and leap.

ETHEL ROHAN
Born and raised in Dublin, Ethel Rohan lives in San Francisco. Her stories and writing often centre on the body — its joys, secrets, memory, urges, splendour, and horrors. When she writes, she's stolen away.

Rohan's first novel, *The Weight of Him*, was published from St. Martin's Press, February 2017, and

from Atlantic Books, June, 2017. *The Weight of Him* won the inaugural Plumeri Fellowship and was named an Amazon Best Book.

She is also the author of two story collections, *Goodnight Nobody* and *Cut Through the Bone*, the former longlisted for The Edge Hill Prize and the latter longlisted for The Story Prize.

Motorcade stops traffic people line the way
Crowds fill Thomond Park The Isle sung
Man woman child sing along
Flags wave the way
Lights guide us home

Orla Foley writes to Anthony Foley

The Flags

The flags droop as the rain pushes them down
Far away a heartbroken crowd ring out The Fields
Disbelief abounds the media waves
Man woman child drown as tears roll down
The light breeze carries the flag flying with ease
Sunshine burns off the torrential rain forecast
An ancient mystical energy encamps the town
Man woman child disbelieving roll by
Every house in town flies the flag
Pubs and houses overflow with mourners
The background buzzing the original sound
Man woman child as one
FR-73* carries the flag
Planes bus the grieving party
Foreign lands friendly faces
Man woman child bring home our brother
Flags drape the coffin
Airport stands guard coffin ushered protectively on
Motorcade stops traffic people line the way
Crowds fill Thomond Park The Isle sung
Man woman child sing along
Flags wave the way
Lights guide us home
Galway Cork Tipperary and Clare they fly everywhere
Man woman child stand together side by side
The flags still fly as does time

The sound of summer fills the town
Life rolls gently by
Man woman child move along
Flags impaled on wire
Faded and torn
Defiantly others fly nine months along
Your widowed bride grieves
Flags tattered worn and shorn
Reminders to those who mourn
Our brother's passed on life lives on
Man woman child life goes on
The wind changes
Flags wave to Thomond Park
Uncertainty about changing guard
Have we the strength to battle on
Man woman child do we still have pride
Flags fly high there is life
Everyman finds strength in his wife
Children will take to their own battlefields
Man woman child can love life
The flags dance on your grave
Waving like synchronized swimmers
In an instant suddenly still
The heartache is not gone.

© Orla Foley (Sept 2017)

WELCOME to the club.... The grief club it what I call us who have suffered the loss of a loved one. Whether it was a sudden death like Anthony, who died from SADS (sudden arrhythmic death syndrome) or a slow progressive illness, no one understands our loss unless you have experienced it.

Anthony died on the anniversary of our grandmother Jane's death. In the midst of the shock of hearing about Anthony's sudden death, the moment I realized this coincidence great peace came over me, knowing our granny Jane would have come to him as he left his body. It was a sign from heaven that all is as it is meant to be. This was part of Anthony's life plan on a soul level, and I know he would never have consciously chosen to leave his beautiful wife Olive and his adored boys Tony and Dan.

At our time of need our community and country did everything to ease the burden of our sorrow. The generosity and kindness knew no bounds. Bus Éireann set up a park and ride service to bus the mourners; Michael O'Leary gave a private Ryanair charter plane to bring home Anthony's body; Press 22 had every photo they had of Anthony at my parents' house within 24 hours of his death; and the prayers of love and mountains of cards people sent carried us on a river of love and healing.

Anthony's death was the greatest sorrow I have ever known, yet it was also one the most beautiful spiritual journeys of my life which continues to this day. Life after the 16th of October 2016 is a different world than before. So many silver linings have occurred. It is ok for Irish men to show emotion and cry. So many men got screened and went for health checks after Anthony's death, and many are alive and well today as a result.

To this day I still cry and that's ok too. The heartbreaking pain I felt in the first year has subsided, yet when we lose another loved one or friend it brings the heartache back as I feel the pain of the ones left behind and know the journey ahead is a hard one. Nobody promised us life would be easy did they?

My promise to Anthony is to keep him alive for his boys. Anytime I remember a story or something he said I share it. Even if its uncomfortable for me it is worth it as their Dad still lives in our memories, of which we are blessed to have many happy ones.

There is a Buddhist story of a bereaved mother begging the Buddha to bring her son back to life. Buddha said, "Yes I can help you". All he would need from her was a simple mustard seed from the nearby village, with one stipulation it had to "be from a house that has not known death". The mother was excited and went house to house search for a family who had been spared yet came back empty handed. As she travelled from house to house she heard story after story of loss of loved ones, her sense of aloneness in her grief subsided. She understood Buddha's help and buried her child with peace. We are never alone in our grief.

ORLA FOLEY
Orla Foley is the youngest sibling of the Killaloe-based rugby Foley clan, who wrote the poem, *The Flags*, as a tribute to her brother, Anthony 'Axel' Foley. A local therapist at Kincora Therapy, Orla loves to keep fit and healthy, and this is reflected in her writings, along with her love of travelling and experience of new cultures and old wisdoms. She studied in the Killaloe Hedge-School of writing in 2005 and then joined the

associated writers group. Orla's poems and prose have appeared in newspapers and online media — *The Limerick Leader, The Star, The Mirror* and *Buzz.ie.*

It broke Dad's heart to fill in your grave with earth, alongside your friends, uncles and cousins, but we knew that your final message had to be carried out that life was precious and death was final.

Elma and Fionnbar Walsh write to Donal Walsh

Dear Donal

WE have been asked to write a letter to you expressing our feelings about our journey since you left us. You said to Brendan O'Connor in the interview, "If, by dying, I am to be a symbol to others of the value of life, then I will be content." And boy what a symbol you have become.

We never knew what would happen after you travelled on in your journey "in the palm of His hand" but you left a legacy that few of your age will ever follow. Would you ever have thought that you still have a reach to over thirty thousand young people each year in Ireland through us visiting schools, parishes and clubs all across the country and even internationally? Would you ever have thought that you would be on the curriculum in every school in Ireland in two different subjects? Would you ever have believed that there would be rooms named after you in every Pieta House and in a number of hospice and hospital facilities?

You once asked Mom: "Will people remember me?" Sometimes we now wish would they ever forget! Sorry, that is not really true. You were a gift to us from the day you were born, and throughout the final years from when you were first diagnosed, you became an inspiration and an educator. Would Dad ever have thought that by making a promise to you in those final hours to do the Legends Cycle, that he would be still on a bike four years later, regularly covering over a hundred kilometres? You are now a bigger pain in the butt for your Dad than when you were around... and sometimes the butt gets really sore.

The year after your passing saw us get many signals from you that you were ok and we are happy for those signs, even if it is us interpreting them. They give us solace but never take away the grief and pain of being separated. You would have loved your funeral and the respect shown to you by your peers, your town and even your nation. It was a time of reverent silent respect as you were carried through the town and as you passed the throngs, totalling nearly ten thousand. They firstly gave you a round of applause and then stood silently. For the three-hour ceremony of your funeral and people offering their condolences, your school friends stood in silent respect for you. You would have been both humbled and proud as the Munster team stood guard of honour and carried your coffin, a service reserved for fellow players or past Presidents. We felt the nation mourn. What a kick you would have gotten when Danny did the funeral Hakka in your honour, and scared some of those there because they didn't understand what was going on. One of the local Garda nearly arrested him but was restrained just in time.

It broke Dad's heart to fill your grave with earth alongside your friends, uncles and cousins but we knew that your final message had to be carried out that life was precious and death was final. There is no social media that can glorify death, and it was your message about the finality of taking ones' life that resonated with so many.

Here we are kid, four years on, and you are still affecting not just those around you but many more far beyond. Little did we know when Patrick O'Donoghue, Dad's boss, called him into his office to speak about something very sensitive, it was the goodwill generated around you and how to harness it for the good of others. We set up the Donal Walsh #Livelife Foundation to keep your message going particularly to your peer age group. A lot of people wanted to back it and support it in very practical ways, principally fundraising. It does not take a hell of a lot of funds to keep the message alive so we had to think long and hard how to honour you in the process of distributing the funds. To date over a half a million has been raised and we have passed on nearly four hundred thousand providing appropriate teenage services and facilities up and down the island.

Quite often in our continued journey we are asked personal questions about you, your faith, our favourite memories of you and were you perfect? Where did you get that faith on your journey we sometimes wonder? Yep, we bargained with God when you were first diagnosed and we are often asked how did we cope. We lost the bargaining side of things but we were able to answer that God did not give a burden too big for the shoulders to carry. You showed such great courage in your journey, and such acceptance of what happened to you, that we felt we had to support you in whatever your journey was to be. We will never forget some of the memories of you training the lads on wet evenings, of studying new moves and training schedules used by the All Blacks and other international squads. Were you perfect, no! But you were someone special. To us you will always be the son who challenged boundaries, who faced challenges, who stuck up for the small guy but at the end of the day you were our son.

It is time to say farewell until we meet again, or until

the next letter or cycle. I know you must be screaming your head off with laughter every time Dad visits the grave dressed in his kit. "Hey, look at that MAMIL (Middle Aged Man In Lycra) my Dad, ha, ha, ha!" Well maybe you are still doing it for us too. Keeping him somewhat fit which he never was before. Then what about Mom? You must be so proud when she stands in front of a whole school to talk about you, just as she did at your funeral in front of a whole nation, the public speaker she has become as a result of your courage. Let us thank you for that. Let the country thank you for being you and starting a conversation that people were afraid of up until your interviews. And let every person who has taken inspiration from you take time to say thanks every now and then.

Each year strangers take time to visit your grave. Some we hear about anecdotally, some leave messages or gifts, and some we never know about. You have been a great influence to many people in the few short years you were with us and you can take comfort in that.

Well we suppose the final mention is, how did you and Axel like the Lions tour last year? We're sure you both had great fun and screamed your heads off just like that night in Thomond in 2008. At least this time it was a draw!

Talk again soon
Love
Mom & Dad

ELMA AND FIONNBAR WALSH
Elma and Fionnbar Walsh are the parents of Donal Walsh, the Kerry teenager whose 19 minutes on

air on the *Saturday Night Show* in 2013, speaking against suicide, had a profound and lasting effect on the nation. Battling cancer for the fourth time, Donal described himself as a 16-year-old with no say in his death sentence, and appealed to young people everywhere not to take their own lives. He asked them to appreciate what they have, and to know that there are always other options, and help is always there. Donal was posthumously awarded the Young Person of the Year Award, and his parents are honouring his legacy with the #LiveLife foundation, which continues to campaign against teenage suicide.

I vividly recall your stricture of
"lies have legs; if you tell one, you'll have
to tell another – so always tell the truth".

Ivan Yates writes to John Francis Yates

Dear Daddy

I've reached the landmark of your death destiny, 57 years. So it's time to update you, compare notes about what happened since; our shared life's lessons; parenting and your lasting impact on me. I always assumed my life expectancy also to be 57, so I've been in a hurry to do things since you departed.

You smoked yourself to death. Your terminal cancer was horrific at the painful end. I succeeded in quitting the fags in 1987 — my greatest personal achievement, given the nicotine addiction. You hated dying so much. I'll never forget you crying on your deathbed, explaining to adolescent me how you knew your terminal fate. I was too immature to fully understand the depth of that saddest conversation. My biggest regret is that we never shared life as adults.

Despite the 38 years since your passing on that desperate Saturday afternoon in February 1979, I surprise myself on how often I think about you. While my life has been and is unrecognisable from those teenage years, your admonitions to me always remained real and relevant. Times have changed, but not your eternal truths.

You instilled in me the deepest sense of family tradition, an immeasurable work ethic, never to be a begrudger; most of all, an insistence upon honesty. I vividly recall your stricture of "lies have legs; if you tell one, you'll have to tell another — always tell the truth". I suppose I've lived my life to crave your approval, without ever knowing if I've earned it.

You denounced my involvement in local politics, fearing it would result in me neglecting my farming responsibilities. Unbelievably, I was elected to the Enniscorthy Urban Council within months of your death and went on to be selected/elected as a Fine Gael Wexford TD in 1981. Your best friend, solicitor and fellow fishermen Des McEvoy, told me how proud you would have been. I had grave doubts that you would have even approved.

Your DNA meant I was always going to go into business. Again, you would have disapproved of bookmaking as a hazardous enterprise. After initial mistakes, Celtic Bookmakers had 17 consecutive years of expansion and profits — reaching a pinnacle of 63 betting shops, 420 employees, €190 million annual turnover and book valuation of €30 million. I failed to heed your repeated long lectures about the peril of bank borrowings.

Ultimately it crashed. I was declared bankrupt in Swansea. Out of the blue, I developed an alternative career in the media as a broadcaster, with roles as radio and TV presenter/pundit/analyst, as well as newspaper columnist. It in turn led to work at a variety of speaking events.

My most important story I have to tell you is that I met the love of my life, a beautiful person, Deirdre Boyd, in Bunclody about a year after you died. She transformed my life. We're married 32 years this year, and have four adult children. My biggest regret is that you've never met your beautiful grandchildren: Andrew; Ciara; Sarah and John. Some of them even have traces of your red hair.

Thankfully, you have been my only insuperable bereavement to date. Your wife and my dearest mother, Mary, is still alive, hale and hearty. Her devotion to you has endured to this day, she hasn't had another partner since. My siblings John, Chris and Val (married to Sean) have led full happy lives locally with two further grandchildren Simon and Jackie.

Our darkest cloud is the precarious future tenure of our family home at Blackstoops. You inculcated ad nauseam into me your adherence to family lineage, me being the sixth generation living here. The farm has been rented out since I became a full-time politician in the early 1980s. Battles with the bank are still ongoing, unresolved and brutally tough. The final outcome is still unclear as I write. The debacle fills me with guilt and remorse. I learned from you to always take responsibility for my mistakes.

It's impossible to explain the pace of change in Ireland today since the 1970s. Enniscorthy doesn't provide employment opportunities for our kids — they're either working in Dublin or abroad. Same applies to Deirdre and myself, with current jobs in Dublin. The Internet is altering every aspect of modern living. Technology is transforming information, life expectancy, convenience, travel and work.

You taught me to appreciate my identity and heritage. Irish society is now rather secular. Protestants have declined numerically; while religion itself is greatly diminished in authority and even relevance amongst the younger generations. I've learned in every walk of life change is constant, with the exception of death being the only certainty.

As to those adult conversations we never had, here goes.

When I came home to farm as a teenager, with a truncated post-primary education upon your insistence, you were both my father and employer. I felt at times, you were unreasonable, even unfair; your old-fashioned views about farming were plainly outdated. After your death, we modernised with mains water supply. I realise now, there were times you were only winding me up.

Also I resented aspects of your parenting: like sending me to boarding school too prematurely, aged eight years; your constant tightness with money; your lack of open displays of love and affection. You were of your time. Undoubtedly, a devoted father; making huge sacrifices to fund our costly private education. Times change. I deliberately tried to be a different father, in these respects.

Your premature passing meant I grew up really fast. It strangely and paradoxically liberated me, at the time, to be my own person.

I am (warts and all) part of your legacy. Thank you, belatedly for everything you've done for me. I'm proud of you and what you stubbornly stood for. I don't know if we'll ever meet again. If not, I'm happy to record in writing, you were without doubt the most profound influence on my life — even beyond the grave.

All my love,

Ivan

IVAN YATES
Ivan Yates is an Irish businessman, broadcaster and former politician. He was elected as a Fine Gael Teachta Dála (TD) representing the Wexford constituency at the 1981 general election and at each election until his retirement from politics in 2002. He served as Minister for Agriculture, Food and Forestry

from 1994 to 1997. He was the founder of the Celtic Bookmakers chain of betting shops.

He currently hosts shows on Newstalk and TV3, and is a regular conference speaker and MC at business events in Ireland.

I was trying, I suppose, to see right through you to the man with the child in his eyes. To the Starman. He was there. In your charm, your eloquence, your understated erudition, your flighty, flirty way of turning a phrase into a yarn.

Helena Mulkerns writes to David Bowie

Dear David,

The news guy didn't quite weep, but his voice was shaky as he told us: David Bowie died this morning ... Nothing mattered for the rest of the day, and for quite some days after that. Which is weird, considering. Somehow it's not right. I have no foundation on which to justify this unexpected grief. I'm part of that media-age mourning process, undignified and first defined when a city paved its streets with flowers for the death of a princess. Following your death, nearly five million Tweets graced a billion screens. I am too sad to Tweet, or to consider the why of it.

The news was like being struck by a spring tide of grief as forceful as if I'd lost a close friend. As if I'd known you all my life. But in a strange way, true to your futuristic sensibility, I have. All the days of my life you have been a companion, a comfort, a musical constant whether on radio or vinyl, digital, ethernet — a presence from another dimension like your own infamous construct, the Starman. Among the myriad of shape-shifts you tricked us through, it was this character, above all, with whom I identified. The Starman, after all, was there all the way from *Space Oddity* (1969), through *Ziggy Stardust* (1973), *Scary Monsters* (1980), *Outside* (1997), then finally and most movingly of all in the video for your swansong *Blackstar* (2016). You played the soundtrack to my life.

You looked quite fragile singing *Starman* on *Top of the Pops*, but provocative as a street punk when you posed on the cover of *The Rise and Fall of Ziggy Stardust* and the *Spiders From Mars*, the first album I ever bought. You presaged — or transcended — every development and trend in popular music in my lifetime and yet throughout your work to the last, there are echoes of old refrains, of familiar sax and guitar riffs, the reappearance of much-loved characters. Through dystopian rock scenarios and dark B-sides you fuelled my teenage angst, at the same time promising that it's all worthwhile.

I remember the first time I saw you, it was possibly 1973. I was a precocious girl, confused by an early puberty and switching channels in search of another David entirely — Cassidy in fact. Suddenly, I was transfixed by a frenzied creature, clad in white satin hot pants and matching boots, throwing shapes all over the screen shocking as Leda's swan. Your gold and crimson make-up glittered, you were all thighs and quivering lips and shameless moves. I remember catching my breath for a reason I didn't quite understand — until I did. I thought you were the sexiest thing I had ever seen. Then I thought — "wait, I don't know if it's a boy or a girl!" Then I thought, I don't care.

In Paris, 1984, I saw you live one summer evening during your *Serious Moonlight* tour. A pivotal gig in my life, I have to say. It's completely your fault that I launched myself that night as an unlikely rock journalist. I danced home on a cloud of you and wrote a review for *Hot Press*. To my surprise, Niall Stokes was encouraging and wanted more. Thank you for the inspiration, David. I had a lot of fun down the years at that caper. All the days I owe you.

Then I finally met you in 1997, as the world was slouching toward the millennium's end. I was to interview you in a Hollywood Gothic hotel off Sunset Boulevard. It was to be a one-on-one, a cover story. I was nervous as I crept up the carpeted stairs to Suite 35. What if you had feet of clay? What if my knees turned to jelly and I fell over? You did not. I did not.

I wasn't under any illusions about the encounter. It would be an artificial conversation, set up by a record company and a magazine. We would discuss your new album and hopefully we might manage a rapport. We did. We spilled over and beyond the project to be promoted into broad-reaching discussion about other arts — music, politics, sexuality, the nascent Internet. You saw how it was changing the world and were already deep in its virtual maze.

I was happy to be there with you, whatever the way of it. I was trying, I suppose, to see through the trickster to the Starman. And he was there. In your charm, your eloquence, your understated erudition, your flighty, flirty way of turning a phrase into a yarn. You were funny and we ended up having a laugh. I was eventually thrown out by your assistant Coco, who called, "It's TIME!" from the room next door, like some disembodied barman. You looked at me and — crazily — I invited you for a pint in the local pub. As if. But you flashed me a twinkle in response and we both laughed. Next time. I took my leave. I was still happy.

So. I spent less than an hour of my whole life with you. Actually talking to you, hearing your voice, smelling your scent (you'd just had a bath and wafted musky bergamot), watching your body moving, fascinated at your newly straightened teeth, tracing along the bones of your hands with my eyes, appreciating their elegance. One hour in my life. But one hour in a life of you.

Can you blame me, for seeing your faker as hero? I was too young for The Beatles and didn't like Disco. Even through Punk and the New Romantics, for me you always had the edge. It was the vaudeville sass of theatre, avant-garde, camp, punk, Brecht, jazz; it was the flamboyance, the sexiness, the wanton cheek of it. Always infused with high-octane emotion, and always in there somewhere, the Starman. Like Shakespeare's Ariel — elusive and lovely and playful and wistful, you were the vulnerable outsider in me, as well as the me that might have been. You were never afraid to dare. From your glam-wild *Lady Stardust* to your Berlin trilogy and the necro-art of *Blackstar*, your overriding impetus has been passion. You understood true androgyny, ever juxtaposing male insolence with female sensuality to produce the best of art. And of course, you were the ultimate time-trickster.

I think that's why, on 10 January 2016, a crowd of shell-shocked people wandered back into the Dublin Bowie Festival venue in the hours following your death announcement, although the event had finished the day before. The place filled up with misguided mourners, then filled up with you — through your music. Clocking the crowd, I understood that this was a vigil for someone who had influenced not just my life, but that of several generations, from post-millennial first-years to erstwhile punks. In the back-to-back videos/films we saw, you didn't seem to have an age. Even days before your death you appeared online laughing, rake thin but apparently joyous: trickster to the last. It's why the ultimate disconnect hit so hard. Our beloved rock star could no longer trick time. Time had been waiting in the wings all along.

Later that night, alone in my car, I watched the videos for your final songs. It was cold, I found *Lazarus* harrowing with its ghastly dance of death where your hand reaches out, shuddering, towards the unknown. *Blackstar* opens with a dead man's foot lying cold on a planet surface, the prone remains of an astronaut trussed up like a patient in a hospital gown, or a space-age shroud. Circled by a Greek Chorus of dancers, you sing blindfolded of that disconnection. And only as the song moves into a second, more tender gear do you bring us up again, one last time, into that high-octane emotion: Something happened the day he died...

Suddenly, I am reminded of an image, not of Starman, but Starchild, the tiny womb-embraced soul immortalised by Stanley Kubrick in his 1968 opus, *2001 A Space Odyssey.*

I know that film influenced you, and I had already recognised the movement of the dying Dr David Bowman reprised by the patient in Lazarus. I don't know what prompted me to connect the iconic star child, but it might have been the way the baby's arm is poised, yet has not yet reached out into life. He/she is about to leave the capsule and to dare, and the image is of eternal potential frozen in purity, timeless and imbued with hope.

It's two years now since you died, and as ever, my heart still turns over when I hear your voice, even half-hidden under the thrum of a busy café, or in a supermarket aisle. For a few seconds, I'm released from the stress or banality of my twenty-first century life, and the darkness that creeps through occasional dreams. I hear your voice and smile. It's a beautiful, light-drenched boy singing *Oh You Pretty Things*. It's a young woman with most of life still ahead of her, ambling around Paris humming *Ashes to Ashes*. It's the man with the child in his eyes, full of all the possibilities we can ever have.

Thank you, David, for the soundtrack to my life.

Love, Helena x

HELENA MULKERNS

Helena Mulkerns is an Irish writer and journalist who has written for *The New York Times*, *Rolling Stone*, *Elle*, *The Irish Times*, *Hot Press* and *The Irish Echo*. She also worked for ten years in UN peacekeeping missions in Central America, Africa and Afghanistan. Her short fiction has been internationally anthologised and shortlisted for the Hennessy New Irish Writing literary awards, America's Pushcart Prize and Ireland's Francis MacManus Short Story Award.

She holds an MA in English Literature and Publishing from NUIG, and has edited two literary anthologies: *Turbulence* and *Red Lamp Black Piano*. She is a recipient of a bursary from the Arts Council of Ireland and her fiction debut, *Ferenji*, a collection of themed short fiction, was published by Doire Press in 2016. In 2018, she appears in the anthology, *Reading The Future* edited by Alan Hayes.

Also see: www.helenamulkerns.com

It was a beautiful morning, a gin clear sky, warm sunshine. On the drive down I was dazed. I phoned my BBC boss and told her you had died. How do you tell anyone your daughter is dead?

John Darvall writes to Polly Darvall

Dear Polly

The night of 30th October 2015 was like so many Friday nights over the last ten years — a long day with my BBC radio show in Bristol, and then on to a late TV shift doing continuity for BFBS in Chalfont St Giles. I always told you life was about graft and that my life was far from glamorous.

I got to the hotel, a good hotel of course, at just after half past midnight. Tired, I went to the bar and ordered a single malt. I took a picture of the whiskey menu to send to Charlotte, as the choice was ridiculous. I missed her as I miss all those I love when I am working away. I went to my room, put on the TV, watched Family Guy, a programme I know you love and, as that finished at around 1.30am, I turned out the light to sleep. It was hard to get to sleep but I thought of all those I love and drifted off. I woke the next morning, went down for a full English, and was disappointed at the quality of what was on offer complete with a cold plate! I resolved to bring it to the attention of the manager. As I always told you and your brother, never be shy at coming forward.

You died when your car hit a tree at 1.30 in the morning of the 31st October. You were going back to my sister's home where you had been living and earning ahead of going to travel the world. That first class degree in Geography you'd attained a few months earlier would have helped, although you could never correctly answer me about some of the world's more obscure capital cities. "It's not about that Dad!" you'd say when I teased you. Your dissertation made me so proud of you, and it brought us back together as you wrote it. You wanted my help. You didn't really need it but we shared its creation. My little girl was a bright, clever, beautiful and funny woman.

After my below par breakfast I went back to my room and my mobile had three missed calls. Two were from your Mum. As usual I thought I'd either upset her (again) or she wanted money for you or Ollie. The other was from my mother. As I couldn't face Sarah shouting at me or asking for money I called my mother, your granny. She asked where I was, I told her, and she told me to sit down. I knew then it was bad news but my first thought was Ollie was in trouble. No.

Granny told me you had been killed in a car accident. She was her usual strong self although I could hear the pain in her voice. My world stopped. It was never to be the same again. It was also the second time in my life that my mother had to tell me somebody close had died. The first time was after my father died, a few days after my eleventh birthday. She told me to go down to my sister's home, where you'd been living. I was distraught. Lost. I didn't know what to do. I phoned Katy. She told me to go down to Southampton so I did. Much like your Mum, you never argue with Katy and she loved you very much too, watching you grow up from five years old.

It was a beautiful morning, a gin clear sky, warm sunshine. On the drive down I was dazed. I phoned my BBC boss and told her you had died. How do you tell anyone your daughter is dead? What is the form of words or the response? I arrived at my sister's house, dazed, where you'd been staying. My strong, loving sister, your Aunt Caroline, crumpled in my arms. After going in to the house, seeing your Mum with Simon, it was still unreal. After all the hugs, the tea drunk, and we left to see you at Southampton hospital.

There you were, looking to the world as if you were asleep but for a bit of glass in your cheek and your head bound in a sheet. You looked beautiful, at peace. I fell to the floor and Ollie, your brave, big brother held me up. I kissed you goodbye and left the room. Then "work me" kicked in as I "interviewed" the poor police officer about what happened to you. Later that day I drove Ollie back to London and I went back to my hotel. The next day I went to work and did my job. I could do that, a bit of "normal". There I was broadcasting around the world, a world that didn't know you were dead. Then I drove to Somerset to be with Katy and your little brother and sister. Nothing was as it was. Nothing is as it was.

So much has changed Polly since you died. I grieve that you will never get to be 23, you will never marry, and you will never prove what I knew to be true about all you are. I grieve for not knowing you well enough. I grieve for our time lost. I grieve for the future you had and what we could have shared, would have shared. I grieve for the 450 people who came to your funeral who miss you every day, and how their lives were touched by you. 450 people Polly!! They loved you. I loved you. I love you. Nothing will ever be as hard for me, Simon, Ollie or Henry than carrying your wicker coffin into the chapel.

So much has changed since you died Polly. I am a member of a club that nobody wants to join, so are your Mum and Simon. The three of us are now great friends. All that anger has gone. We are united in our love for you. We've had dinner together and I've stayed over at the home you grew up in. They are wonderful, beautiful people and I can see why you were the woman you were. I'm now close to Ollie, something you always wanted. I'm now close to my mother, your granny. You did that. I'm honest, true and clear. You did that. You gave me so much joy in life and in your death you have given me even more.

My only wish is that I could share what I have learned since you have gone. You'd be amazed. You would also be trying to work out the angle too! There isn't one. Your death changed me and will continue to do so. Your loss is our compete loss yet your life changed me from the moment you were born in October 1993 and this will continue after your death in October 2015.

Thank you Polly, for every single day you are with me. I know you'd appreciate all the changes. Just one last thing; please come home, we all miss you.

Love,
Dad xxx

JOHN DARVALL

John Darvall is the voice behind BBC Radio Bristol's weekday morning topical phone in, heard around the world on BFBS TV, the service for UK armed forces overseas. A BBC Journalist and Presenter for many years, he has written very poignantly about

insensitive media coverage of families who experience sudden loss.

His 22-year-old student daughter Polly was killed in a car accident in October 2015.

Indulge yourself. Cry out loud. Cry in a low voice. But, cry. And afterwards, put on your make up and go out and face life again.

Mary O'Rourke writes to Enda O'Rourke

Hello Enda

I know full well that's not the correct way to start a letter. One should say 'Dear'. But, because it's you, and because it's me, I'm saying 'hello' to you.

The purpose of this letter to you is for a very good cause and I know you will understand that. So often in our life together you used to gently chide me, and say you are being taken in by such and such a person, such and such a cause. But I would always resist any advice you would give in that regard.

Now Enda, let me explain quite clearly. You and I were married on 14th September 1960 in the Ballybay Parish Church, Kiltoom, Athlone and afterwards, at the Hodson Bay Hotel, Athlone. You died on 30th January 2001 in the Mater Hospital, Dublin. So, in between, we had forty years and four months of a great life together.

We all gathered in Coosan cemetery in Athlone on the day of your burial. But I have never believed that you, Enda O'Rourke, is in that grave. Yes, your body may be gently composting away, but the spirit of Enda O'Rourke is alive and well and going around the ether and, from time to time, coming to say hello to me or to give good advice.

Now in case anyone gets up in arms, I do believe there is a God, because I do believe the world would not be able to function and operate the way it does without an all-seeing hand. But my other belief is that those we love dearly are never cut off from us but remain — not within touchable distance — but within advice distance, and within the spirit of how we had lived together.

Those forty years and four months seem so long and yet were so short. I was twenty-three and you were twenty-five the day we got married and we were truly young and innocent in the ways of life.

What I always loved about you Enda was that you were always there for me and, in the world of politics into which I entered, that was such a bountiful gift, to have someone close to me, who knew me so well and was able to advise and help in so many ways.

When I first met you Enda, a few years short of 1960, what I admired first about you was your looks. I always think that's how a couple really get together. They like how the other looks and from that grows lust and from lust grows love. And that's the way it will always be I guess. I loved your dark good looks, I loved your manner and I loved how we got on very quickly when we got together, and how very quickly we became so fond of one another. In our day, as you know, even though we skirted close to the edge, we never went over it. In our day that was regarded as being 'for the wedding night' so to speak. It's all different now but still, looking back on it, I never regretted that we were good in that sense of the word.

I remember coming back into our home a few days after the funeral. I had gone back to Cabinet and to the Dáil within three days of the funeral and then, the following Thursday/Friday I came home here for my first weekend without you.

I will always remember, and it is seared in my brain, coming into the house on my own. I was a member of Cabinet at the time and my nice Garda driver had left me at the house. I walked into the living room and immediately what struck me was the total quietness and silence. I remember thinking of the song 'Is That All There Is,' and I knew immediately that I was staring into an abyss of loneliness and solitude.

So, what did I do Enda? Well, you know what I did. I went down to our bedroom and I turned on the radio. I went into the little office I had and I turned on the radio, and I came into the kitchen/living room and I turned on the radio. So wherever I went in the house there were noises, voices and music. It felt that there was somebody around and that I wasn't in that well of widowhood on my own.

Life quickly resumed its even pattern. Saturday was an all-day clinic day as it always was. A very dear friend and neighbour came over and helped me with the clinic, answering the door and seeing people in. Tasks you had done so voluntarily and so joyfully for me during my political years.

As you know Enda, I was also lucky in that our great friends, Míchael and Maura, remained my dear friends and, to this day, they are my best friends in life. We always went out on a Saturday night and we quickly resumed that pattern. Both Aengus and Feargal were away living in Dublin. Feargal was married and Aengus was going steady with a lovely girl, Lisa, whom he later married.

But I had huge wells of loneliness. Yes, there was the pattern to life and yes, there were the voices and music in the house and yes, there were friends and family. But I got into bed on my own. I got out of bed in the morning on my own. Do you remember Enda how we used to talk in the mornings together? I would bring in a cup of tea to you and I would bring in my own cup of tea and we would sit and have that close chat to one another. Chat, interlaced with love and feeling and a close warmth which I have never experienced since you passed away.

The odd thing is, that even though I had these patches of deep loneliness, I didn't want to bring back that warmth again. It could never be replaced with anyone else. It could never be the same unless it was with you, lovely darling Enda.

I missed all the practical things you did for me. You sorted out all our finances. You paid the bills when they were due. You came with me shopping to the supermarket. You didn't come in, but you were there in the car when I came out with my bundles and we planned things together. I often found myself pulling up short and wondering and saying 'now what would Enda do if he was here?' when a difficulty presented itself. And somehow, because you are in the spirit around, the difficulties usually resolved themselves.

Over time, the sense of desolation and loss lessened but the gap in my life, the comforting voice and personal warmth became more acute and I never lost that sense, from time to time, of utter desolation.

I lost my seat in 2002, due, in no small way to the fact that I missed you watching out for me. You would be up in the local pub, you would be in town, knocking around, and you would pick up vibes which I, in my isolation, could not pick up. You know the way men can do these things and somehow, still, women can't. Be that as it may, I lost my seat, went on into the Seanad, back into the Dáil, family got married, had children, so life went on in a good routine.

Oh! Enda! I always regret that you never met our grandchildren. You would have loved them, spoiled them, indulged them and they would have been, as they are for me, the light of your life. I know that you would be watching out for them, you would be thinking of them. You would be so happy to see life renew itself again which is the glad, joyful feeling I have when I look at any of our grandchildren, or when I talk to any of them. It is life again.

In fact, Enda, it was the coming of grandchildren — two to Feargal and Maeve in Dublin (Jennifer and Sam), four to Aengus and Lisa here in Athlone (Luke, Sarah, James and Scott) — it was the coming of all those lively, bright-faced, wonderful new beings that made me, if you like, get out of my oft-times sloughs of despair. I would hear the key at the door, and in would come one or other, or maybe all four, of the Athlone grandchildren and life would be lit up with the possibilities of the future.

They all know you Enda because every year we have a remembrance family Mass for our family and friends — all the people who knew us together. Afterwards, we have a lunch in the house and the children know that it is 'Enda's Party Day'. I stumbled on the idea and I'm so glad I did because I can see that somehow you, an absent grandfather, have become real to them. And I often hear them saying 'When is Enda's party day?' and 'Who will be at Enda's next party day'? It's amazing.

As I write these words I am crying but, Enda, they are not cries of despair. In a way, they are cries of joy as I think back to all the happy times we had together. In case people reading this think we lived in cloud cuckoo land, we didn't. There were ups and downs as there are in any family. There were rows and making up as there are in any family, but we were always able to come together in love again.

I strongly encourage anyone who has had a great loss to cry, to cry deeply about it. Don't mind if you seem to despair, you won't be. In the crying, will be the memories and the memories will be laced with love and happiness, so cry. Indulge yourself. Cry out loud. Cry in a low voice. But, cry. And afterwards, put on your make-up and go out and face life again.

So, Enda, we will meet again. I know we will. Not physically, but in spirit. You will meet my spirit and my spirit will meet you and we will be the same in spirit as we were in life. I don't know if we'll talk together, but our spirits will be together and we will be in happy memory of all of our forty years and four months together.

So, goodbye for now Enda. I still miss you so much but, much more than that, I cherish the memories of my years with you since Mary Lenihan married Enda O'Rourke.

See you soon Enda (after all I am 80 now)

Love Mary

MARY O'ROURKE
Mary O'Rourke is a well loved former politician who served for many years at the highest levels in Irish politics for the Fianna Fail party. She was Leader of Seanad Éireann and Leader of Fianna Fáil in the Seanad from 2002 to 2007; Deputy Leader of Fianna Fáil from 1994 to 2002; Minister for Public Enterprise from 1997 to 2002; Minister for Health and Children

from 1991 to 1992 and Minister for Education from 1987
to 1991. She is now a regular contributor to Irish radio
and television.

> *I have learned so very much in the last four years... mostly I have learned it is possible to live with a broken heart. And that it is possible to make that life meaningful. You inspire me every day to continue to live and not just exist.*

Kathleen Chada writes to Eoghan and Ruairi Chada

Dear Eoghan and Ruairi

Can I just start this by embarrassing you both....my right as a mother. Despite what you always tell me, you may be big boys now but you will always be my babies and that will never change no matter how old you are or where you are.

And know I will always be your Mom, always.

So much has changed since you left me over four years ago now. I just hope that you can be proud of me and of the woman and mother I continue to be. Every day without you feels like an eternity, and yet it passes in a blink. And every day I get through is for you both. Someday it may even be for me.

These last four years have been the worst of my life. Such a contrast to the previous ten which were the best when you first arrived Oe and then you Ru to make our family complete. From the first positive test you were both loved and that continues for an eternity. You both made life complete for me, and despite the pain now, I would never ever not have wanted you in my life. It is a privilege to call you my sons.

I am so incredibly proud of you both; for the boys you were, the men you would have become, and the angels I know you are today — looking down and watching over all those you love. You continue to inspire me and so many of your family and friends, to live and appreciate our lives more every day. To quote one of your cousins, 'I believe that you were born perfect and that God just waited for the right moment to take you into his arms'.

I just love the thought behind that. Your cousins miss you so much. They have lost something so very precious in having you there to guide them Oe, and Ru to instigate the mischief.

I do have to ask why God chose you both. I mean I understand why he would want you both, but why then??

I have learned so very much in the last four years. Mostly I have learned that it is possible to live with a broken heart. And that it is possible to make that life meaningful. You inspire me every day to continue to live, and not to just exist. That I can smile and be happy. It does not mean I miss you less but that you help me to be the person I am and want to be.

I know that you are with me always just as I know that a few months ago I had to let you go. That to try to hold on was not fair to you both. Just as I know by doing this I get to keep you inside me. This way I just had to develop a new way of being with you. And I know wherever you are, you are together and looking after each other and that helps a little. You were so close in life, why would that be any different now?

I love you both to the moon and back and round the world and back again. And I love you more than that again — no limits. Thank you for being my boys. For choosing me to be your Mom and to continue to be your Mom. You will always be my greatest achievements and I am so incredibly proud to be your Mom, always.

Mmmm... ah

KATHLEEN CHADA

Kathleen Chada is a nurse who has spent all her working life supporting families to realise their dream of having a baby. She is a key member of the IVF team at the Rotunda Hospital.

Her son Eoghan was born in 2002 followed by Ruairi in 2008. The boys were very close and loved living in Ballinkillen, the home of Kathleen's childhood, growing up in a close knit community, and surrounded by a loving extended family.

The boys' father, Sanj Chada, is serving a life sentence for abducting and killing the boys in 2014.

Kathleen has spoken out about the impact of murder on families, and is a founder member of SAVE, Sentencing and Victim Equality, which will campaign for changes to sentencing.

I'm still trying to entertain people by running a TV company and now we are making a show, Dancing With the Stars, that I know you would have loved, as one of my earliest memories is of you going to ballroom dances.

Larry Bass writes to Patricia Bass

Dear Mum

June 1977 is another lifetime ago, so I've a lot to update you on.

When you left us I was 12, Tony was 13, but Sharon was only 7 and left in a house with all men!! Poor Sharon had to deal with three grumpy men growing up. Dad was in a bad place for a long time, but I guess having to work all day and get home and look after three kids and a house, with two of us becoming teenagers, gave him plenty of life to worry about.

He was a mighty Dad who did what he could to give us what we needed; what we wanted was another matter. The only way we got what we wanted was to work for it. I had started work early, as you know before you died, in the garage next door. But I then also started working in the hotel across the road and started doing discos. So getting out and fending for ourselves gave us a sense of independence early, and we all just got on with life and made our day to day decisions from an early age. So thanks Mum, you gave us a great start in life. You also gave us a clear understanding of right and wrong.

Life was busy when you left us, and that helped us get through without you, but I never forgot you, and in fact I find myself thinking of you more and more these days. It has been a whirlwind of ups and downs since '77, but I know you have got me through the dark days by always being there with me.

My biggest regret is that you never got to meet my beautiful wife Catherine, who has made my life complete. In fact until I met Catherine, there was a huge void after you passed. I know you would have loved her, and you two would have been the best of friends.

You would also have doted over our four fab kids — Carla who is now 23 and finished college and working; Grace who is in 3rd year of an engineering degree; Robert who has started a degree in film and TV — I've no idea why!! — and Lauren who will need your help soon to do her Leaving Cert. They are all great kids and they would have loved you as they now love Dad. They idolise him when he comes to visit.

Dad — Paddy — who is soon to be 88 and still going strong, maybe a little slower, but we still can't get him to stop the gardening around your home in Derrybawn, and driving up and down to Avoca, where he visits you regularly. He has taken over the praying from you, and spends huge time down in the church.

I'm still trying to entertain people by running a TV company and now we are making a dance show, *Dancing With The Stars*, that I know you would have loved. One of my earliest memories is of you going to ballroom dances. Funny how life brings us back.

I miss you everyday Mum, you left a hell of a legacy.
Love you lots always,
Larry

(Oh I forgot, no one calls me Laurence now, that was what you called me)

LARRY BASS

Larry Bass is the award winning producer of Ireland's best loved television programmes — *Dancing With the Stars, Dragons' Den, The Voice of Ireland, Master Chef, Home of the Year, The Apprentice* and many more. He is the founder and CEO of Shinawil Productions and one of the most influential figures in Irish television in recent years. He has served on the Boards of the Broadcasting Authority of Ireland, Screen Training Ireland, Screen Producers Ireland and on the jury of the International Emmys.

His mother, Patricia (Pat) Bass née Byrne, died on June 8th, 1977, aged 42 years.

"....the dress I wore when I got my first kiss, these and many more are all there, the stories of our lives in fabric... We all have something special to remember you by: mine is that patchwork quilt."

Ann O'Loughlin writes to Anne O'Loughlin

Dear Mam

Remember that summer we made the patchwork quilt? I was 15 years old and you must have been fed up of a teenager moping around the house. I loved sewing with you, the shared moments over a shared endeavour, not that I took time then to tell you.

A conscientious dressmaker you approached each task in a considered careful fashion, pinning down the tissue pattern, following instructions, sewing long seams without stopping. Nearly always you changed the pattern, chalking out the changes directly on to the fabric, before tacking the garment together.

Oh, how I hated wasting time tacking. You were not one for giving out, you smiled and said "You will live and learn my lady." I did when I had to rip, stitch by stitch, a long seam I had recklessly machined without one tacking thread to keep it even. But back to the quilt. I pretended at first I wasn't interested, saying I would prefer to go to the lake with my friends. You did not take umbrage, but instead asked me to help with boxes and bags of fabric you had carefully stored away on the top shelf of the hot press.

You had fashioned the most beautiful outfits for your three daughters over the years, but what we did not know was the leftover swatches you squirrelled away. Opening the boxes, the history of our lives was spread in colourful pieces of fabric you had lovingly ironed and folded away.

As we waded through the fabric, the memories flooded

back. Working side by side, I think back now on many precious moments together, sometimes we laughed at the light funny stories thrown up by the fabric, sometimes we cried to think of loved ones passed away.

All my dresses were there, those which had been fashioned from a McCall or Butterick pattern, or the dresses run up in an evening for a surprise school event the next day.

There was the lilac fabric with the tiny purple hearts, a dress that had been run up in a jiffy and worn with pride on a school sports day, until I fell over during the three legged race, tearing the dress up the side. I remember I was so upset and full of wounded pride, I refused to wear the dress ever again, even after you stayed up late to unpick the side panel and carefully replace it with another of the same fabric.

There was the soft pink with white flowers made for my step out of independence. I was allowed to get the train on my own to Dublin to stay in Michael's first house. The floral fabric touched with gold sent in a parcel from Auntie Mary in America. It meant I was the first for miles around to have a dress with a fashionable deep ruffle at the hem and an off the shoulder gathered frill. The strip of rich silk from a skirt Auntie Mary sent in another parcel, refashioned into a mini. No matter what length you allowed, once out the door the skirt was rolled up to an indecent length.

The royal blue dress with a delicate flower Mary wore for her first date with her future husband, the bridesmaid dresses you sewed for your daughters' weddings, summery, floral with a light edging of velvet; the dress I wore when I got my first kiss, these and many more are all there, the stories of our lives in fabric.

Mam, you passed away two years ago, your five children

at your bedside. We kept vigil sharing our memories. We each had a special story to tell, we laughed and cried. The memories sustain us now. We all have something special to remember you by: mine is that patchwork quilt.

Now, as I run my hand over the patchwork quilt, I am so happy you persuaded me to do it. When life is throwing its worst, when everything else is wrong, I have the quilt, my blanket of memories to sustain me.

Making the patchwork quilt was a giant labour of love when not only did we cement our mother daughter relationship, but we also became good friends. Now is a fitting time to say thank you for the precious memories which sustain me every day.

Love, Ann xx

ANN O'LOUGHLIN

A leading journalist in Ireland, Ann O'Loughlin has covered all major news events of the last three decades. Ann spent most of her career with Independent Newspapers where she was Security Correspondent at the height of The Troubles, and a senior journalist on the *Irish Independent* and *Evening Herald*. She is currently a senior journalist with the *Irish Examiner* newspaper. Ann has also lived in India. Originally from the west of Ireland she now lives on the east coast with her husband and two children. Ann's first book *The Ballroom Café* was a bestseller as was her second novel, *The Judge's Wife*. Ann's third book *The Ludlow Ladies Society* is out now.

Ann's letter is to her mother, Anne O'Loughlin, who passed away in May 2015. Anne was in her late 80s when she died.

*You were a son. You were a brother.
You were a cousin. You were a schoolmate.
You were a neighbour. You were a friend.
You were a little boy. Most importantly...
You will never be forgotten.*

Kevin Kuster writes to Kurt Kuster

Dear Kurt

I remember when I heard the news.
You were the first person in my life that passed away.
I was too young to understand the concept of death.
You were too young to go so soon.

I could not comprehend the magnitude of not seeing you
once more.
You have never been seen again although you are often felt.

I did not grasp how your departure would forever change
so many.
You have been reunited with a few. Someday you will be
reunited with all.

I think of you frequently but failed to understand how significant your loss would be.
Your passing had a tremendous impact on everyone who
encountered you.

I and many grieved your departure.
You left way too quickly. No time for goodbyes.
Some recovered. Some did not. Some still wear the emo-
tional scars of losing you.

I am significantly older.
You are still 12 years old.

I and many people wonder what great things you would have accomplished in life.
You left a lasting impression.

You left and your passing forever changed so many lives.

You were a son.
You were a brother.
You were a cousin.
You were a schoolmate.
You were a neighbour.
You were a friend.
You were a little boy.
Most importantly...
You will never be forgotten.

Kevin

Kurt Kuster 1963-1976
My cousin Kurt was only 12 when he suddenly died. Although I was only 8 years old, I remember the morning and moment vividly when my father told me he had passed. Kurt died from a very rare virus called Reyes Syndrome. (It's an infection to the liver connected with chickenpox.)

Forty-one years later there was a second re-dedication memorial service at his Long Branch NJ grade school honouring his life. Several of his schoolmates, family and friends attended the replanting of a memorial tree that had been removed due to construction. With the new school finally completed, Kurt's memorial tree and plaque were planted again and re-dedicated in his honor 41 years later.

It is an amazing testimony to his short life that so many would gather and be so motivated to ensure his life and memory were not forgotten.

As I reflected on Kurt's passing and thought about the re-dedication, I am painfully aware that my son, Kaedin, just tuned 13. No parent should ever have to bury a child. I cannot image the pain and sorrow that my aunt, uncle and cousins all experienced losing a child and brother so young and so suddenly. My father rarely talked of my cousin's death. However, on the rare occasion that he did, he would always say, "My brother Billy was never the same." I have learned there is no forgetting the death of a loved one. Why or how could you. You just slowly heal by allowing those around you to love, support and care for you one day at a time for the rest of your life.

Kurt was a special kid. There was a joyful, engaging, funny and magnetic quality about him. One time when we were visiting, without anyone knowing it, Kurt went into the bathroom, put on a wig, snow white cold cream on his face and put on a bra stuffed with toilet paper. When he came out of the bathroom to perform for my sister and I, it was the funniest and naughtiest thing our young eyes had ever seen! We didn't know what to do with ourselves and prayed that no one came into the room to see us laughing with him prancing around.

Although you have been missed by so many for so long, Kurt, it's obvious to me that some stars burn so bright and bring so much joy, it's impossible for them to remain as long as we all would have liked. You are in my thoughts and prayers and I thank you for looking over all of us since you left.

Dedicated to my Aunt Nina, Uncle Bill, and cousins, Karen, Billy, Kim and Brian.

KEVIN KUSTER

Kevin Kuster is a renowned international photographer who spent 18 years as the Director of photography for the Playboy Group. He has worked with Oscar-winning directors and has produced photographs for some of the biggest celebrities in Hollywood, professional sports, politics and world events.

Currently, he is the Creative Director for Watts of Love, a global solar lighting non-profit dedicated to providing lights to the poorest homes in the developing world. He is also CEO of #JJ, the world's largest Instagram community with over 640,000 followers. His work with #JJ has been featured by *The New York Times* and *Newsweek*. Kevin speaks regularly at major events like Macworld on the power of social media and brand building.

You would have been so very, very talented at living a long and useful life. But you didn't get to, did you? Thirty-two years old, and your time was up, and we'll never know why.

Orlaith Carmody writes to Kieran Gleeson

Dear Kieran

So here we are, a little shy of thirty years. Can you believe it? Thirty years since you squeezed my hand one last time, gently and deliberately let it go, and reached weakly for the bell on a cord that lay on the cover of the Hospice bed. Ring that damn bell I thought fiercely as my tears scalded. Keep ringing it all the way there. Tell them you are coming. Make them open the gates wide and give you the welcome you deserve; the welcome you have earned hard over three and a half years with smiles, strength, gentle philosophy, tolerance, humour and good grace.

You sighed a little sigh, and now at this remove I don't know if I imagined it, but I thought I saw you smile and give yourself up with even more of that good grace. And it was over.

My Mam and Dad and my sister were there for me, as were your brother and his lovely wife, numb and shocked beyond belief, but paddling furiously, working with the Hospice team on soothing and smoothing. Nothing was rushed. Tea drunk right there in the room with you, lots of lovely words said. And then at some stage a suggestion that we might go home to bed and deal with it all in the morning.

I must have walked outside to the car on some invisible conveyor belt; gazing up at the cold heavens, breath laboured, vaguely taking some comfort from that old notion that there was one more star up there, twinkling in the frosty night.

Then waking a few hours later punch drunk, savage awareness smothering, overwhelming, crippling. Family all around me whispering, caring, loving. It was so bloody hard.

But I kept remembering how you had been. How you had pondered each new indignity imposed upon you, month after month, and consciously decided you could do it, you could suck it up and make it all work. And boy did you make it work.

Do you remember sitting on that lovely bench in France, puffing on a cigar, saying this is the life, trying out snails and beautiful wines and madly calorific pastries? How they said we should never be so bold as to try a holiday in France; the ferry, the AA yellow stickers turning the car beams the other way, the wheelchair borrowed from Fannin Health-care. We would come a cropper, guaranteed. It would all end in tears.

I never told them that it nearly did. When you crashed to the floor in the bathroom of the beautiful *gîte*, and I had to run screaming to the Madame next door for help. But thankfully only a few horrible bruises and we were on the way from Normandy to Paris, finding the Eiffel Tower all by ourselves, long before SatNav, me driving our Renault 5 like a native and you plotting the route with the computer analyst's attention to detail.

If you only knew where the IT world you loved has come to now. Social media and emails pinging around the planet at the speed of light. All our shopping and travel bookings done online.

And the motorway system all over the country! The first one in Naas was built in 1983 the year we were married. We marvelled at it as we drove down to Limerick to spend weekends with your folks. When I drive home now along the quays in Dublin to the port tunnel I think of you as I pass the tall glass buildings. The dereliction that used to be there. You wouldn't recognise the city now. It is bright and buzzy and active. You would absolutely love it. I regularly feel so sad about all the things you missed.

Now here is something completely weird. I sometimes have this bizarre fantasy that you didn't die that time. That something happened to us and what we had together, and we ended up separating, as happens to so many. You went your way and I went mine, and you are now living happily somewhere the other side of town with your wife and family. I imagine what they would look like, what your life would be. And I always see you smiling, growing older elegantly, still enjoying your garden, your cigars, your rugby, your tennis; keeping your car immaculate, calmly dealing with whatever work or family crises came your way. You would have been so very, very talented at living a long and useful life.

But you didn't get to, did you? Thirty-two years old, and your time was up, and we'll never know why, *Don't Go* from the Hothouse Flowers playing off the air that year, breaking my heart over and over and over again.

So, what happened to me? Almost a year to the day after you left, someone I was working with, who I had become very close to, took me out for coffee one morning and announced that I was going to be the mother of his children. And only you will fully know what that will have meant to me. The chance we never had.

Gavin is very different to you, but you would get on like

a house on fire. You would just love each other's sense of humour, and completely respect each other's work ethic.

We have been so lucky in the love we found, our four beautiful children, our work, our common purpose. We will be married twenty-five years this Spring, which seems extraordinary.

Kieran, you and I were still honeymooners when things changed so awfully for us, so we have no way of knowing how it would have worked out. But I can tell you there are many, many ups and downs on the road in a long relationship, no matter how strong. And if I have learned anything, it is that we all have to keep believing that there are good things around the corner, just as you always did.

So here is the main thing. Your extraordinary ability to deal with what was happening to you made me the person I am today. I watched you learn to write with your left hand, begin walking with a stick, and then to use a wheelchair. You lost your hair, your fine physique, part of your sight. And every time, you made it work for you, for us, for everyone who met you, by being such great company, by being so patient, accepting, resilient. I am so grateful that I got to spend those years with you and to learn so much from you.

When I became engaged to Gavin, he asked could we have the stones from your ring made into the new one, so you could come on the journey with us. It has been that way always; you are with us.

And finally, something that you will absolutely love. You have three children named after you! Your nephew, your great nephew — who also features in this book — and my nephew — Dearbhla's lad. That is some legacy.

I miss you still, Orlaith

ORLAITH CARMODY

Orlaith Carmody is the editor of *Without You — Living With Loss*. She was widowed at the age of 28 when her first husband, Kieran Gleeson, passed away at Harold's Cross following a three and a half year struggle with a brain tumour. She has always wanted to honour his memory, and celebrate the work of the Hospice, and this book is the fulfillment of that wish.

A communications consultant, journalist and broadcaster, Orlaith is the also the author of *Perform As A Leader*. She lives on the Louth/Meath border with her husband Gavin Duffy and four children, now young adults.

You took responsibility for the family farm with nothing to work with other than a wheelbarrow, sledge, shovel, crowbar ~ and a disability.

Declan Breathnach writes to Brendan Breathnach

Dear Dad

My earliest memories of you centre around family, faith, farming and friendship. The 8th of December, the farmers' Christmas, was very special as we traipsed to Dublin annually for a family day out. And being the only son, and heir, I was your valet and bag-carrier, while Mam took the girls shopping. You always had two shops to visit — Arnotts to be fitted for a new suit, and Easons where you bought an educational book for every niece and nephew on both sides of the family. You loved Christmas and your role in the pudding making was a sight to behold. We helped Mam with the mixing — eating as much of the mix as we could — while you directed proceedings. You lined the old tin sweet cans, as many as 30 of them, and secured the lids so water wouldn't get in while they steamed in our garage. The puddings were presents, not just for neighbours, but for family and friends worldwide.

I remember our visits to Granda where an oil lamp lit up my historical initiation. Pearse, Connolly, De Valera and Clarke looked on as Granda expanded on their achievements and ambitions for the new Ireland, while eating the dinner we delivered every day. You left me to entertain him, or be entertained, while you tended the livestock.

You had a passion for politics which stemmed from your own parents, Bernard and Annie Walshe, both active in the Old IRA and Cumann na mBan. But you never allowed your well-known support and loyalty to Fianna

Fáil to interfere with your civil service role as County Registrar and Returning Officer. You took up the role of County Registrar in 1960 when you were 37, noted in the newspapers of the time as the youngest in Ireland to hold this office.

You had a huge grá for St. Brides GFC and served as Treasurer for more than 50 years and also chaired the Louth County Board. One great friend recalls your love of detail, and said the cost of a stamp would be queried, in either direction, whether you were owed the cost or that cost was due to be paid by you.

For me, I did try my best at football, but I couldn't kick snow off a rope so left that to the professionals! But your influence and that of Mam on the community did stem from your daily attendance at Mass and devotion to the rosary, which did of course shape my views on the importance of loyalty to the church and state, respect for oneself, family, community, county and country. I think my passion for community development came directly from you.

In writing this most difficult piece it is hard to capture you, the man, but I think your approach was to try to succeed without being pushy, or forward, or in your face. Words that come to mind for you are humility, respect, understanding and problem solving. My biggest regret is that you were not alive to see me elected to Dáil Éireann, having mentored and advised so many TDs in their own careers — Frank Aiken, Joe Farrell, Padraig Faulkner, Rory O'Hanlon and Seamus Kirk. Coincidently three of your protégées went on to become the Ceann Comhairle!

I hope the fact that I now rent your original solicitor practice office at 16 Earl Street in Dundalk brings you some satisfaction. It continues not just to be nostalgic, but it is like walking in your footsteps every day.

I could not write to you Dad without mentioning your environmental and farm enterprise, another huge influence on me. With your great friends Nicholas Marry and Pat O'Neill you brought water to the Knockbridge Community in the first water scheme project that saw the village expand and grow to what it is today. You couldn't know that years later I would become secretary to the largest water scheme in Louth, to deliver an infrastructure critical to the development of the county.

Your love for farming came at an early age when a very serious leg injury playing football left you at home and out of education for seven years. You took responsibility for the family farm with nothing to work with other than a wheelbarrow, sledge, shovel, crowbar — and a disability.

Many may not appreciate the hardship in agriculture at the time, but you know there was no tractor but a piece of plastic tied to the back bumper of the old car to drag bales to feed outlying stock. My uncle Enda sat with a fiddle — not the musical type — spreading clover seed to replace the nitrogen in the soil, and you often deposited him in the field along with the seed as you bumped along.

You would always say that we are custodians of the environment, as you would carefully pick ragwort in your slow way, so the seeds would not spread to neighbouring farms. I know I have inherited that legacy.

It is extraordinary that despite the education you missed, and the work of the farm, that you got yourself ready for the Law Society exams, and passed with flying colours, taking first place and the Silver Medal in 1948. Your determination was exceptional, and I have often smiled proudly at the wall of honour in CBS Dundalk, where your photo is placed to recognise your achievements in education. Your grandson Cian passed it every day while he attended CBS too.

I think that despite a certain perception of your work status, you struggled as so many of us do these days to give your family a quality of life and a good education, and to keep yourself and Mam's heads above water. At one stage you had four of us in third level education, which can't have been easy.

You had a serious work ethic, and while I was studying to be a national school teacher I had to come home every weekend, without any wages, to help your struggle to keep the family farm going. You can imagine how impressed I was with that. Then the day I qualified, you opened a drawer in your desk and gave me a bank deposit book. You had lodged £5 for every animal I had helped with over the years. "This will help you buy your first car", you said. Tears filled my eyes as I realised that there was £1,500 in the account, a huge amount of money at the time. And it did buy the car.

The final memory I want to talk to you about Dad is our annual summer holidays in the Neptune Hotel in Bettystown, some of the young people staying in the Crimmons house beside the hotel in an attempt by you and Mam to shade us from 'that growing drink mentality'. They were great times as all and sundry visited from the wider family and friends circle. You carried the cost of the whole thing, knowing that the memories would be priceless for everyone. You were so right. Bettystown in its heyday was a special treat. My memories of it are privileged and precious.

The late Frank Sinatra said in a song 'Regrets I have a few but then again too few to mention'. In truth those regrets are because of an era where to say 'I love you' was not a thing for many, including me. I didn't realise until very late my appreciation for your love, guidance, direction and inspiration. I didn't get to say 'I love you' until 3 weeks before you died. I am so glad I did.

Ar dheis Dé go raibh a anam dilis

DECLAN BREATHNACH

Declan Breathnach, TD, is from Knockbridge, Dundalk and is the father of two adult children, Cian & Meabh. He was formerly a Primary School Principal at Walshestown NS, Clogherhead and taught before that in Dunleer NS. Declan has been a member of Louth County Council for over 25 years serving as Chairperson on two occasions and he was the first Chair of Dundalk Municipal District. He is a lifelong community activist with interests in Tidy Towns, tourism promotion, community development, farming and employment. He was elected to Dáil Éireann in 2016.

*You died in dignity as you had lived,
a most elegant woman, a devoted mother and
a Lady to your perfectly manicured fingertips.
I will carry on your graceful legacy as
best I can and live well in your honour.*

Olivia Tracey writes to Maura Tracey

Dear Mammy

I know that you're gone, yet it seems like you're not. Maybe it's because you only passed away six months ago, and so the reality of the loss hasn't hit home, or I simply feel your presence around me. It's probably both. You are still here, albeit in spirit, and that's a great comfort to me.

I miss your physical presence so much, our phone calls across the miles. But I talk to you on a regular basis, especially when I'm at home in the living room. "Good morning Mammy. Another sunny morning in LA". I glance over from the couch or dinner table at your beautiful picture gracing the hall table. That picture really affects me. You seem so alive behind the glass, your eyes sparkling, a little tear nesting in one, catching the light like a diamond. I hope it's a happy tear.

You looked magnificent on the day that picture was taken. It was Stephen and Leagh's wedding, March 20th 2010, on a sunny, though brisk day in Aughrim, Co. Wicklow. I remember you wore that silver grey knit two-piece — long slim skirt, perfectly coordinated with a winter-white knit jacket. The jacket was from Dunnes but on you, it was like Dior. The two-piece had been Helen's. Of course you also had your pearls and that beaded hair netting that invisibly kept your groomed do in place. Remember Janice, my LA makeup artist friend from Navan? She was always fascinated with that beaded net. "Oh your mother" she'd say, "and the little diamonds in her hair. She's like royalty."

It's true. You were like royalty, especially in this picture. It's hard to believe that you were only two months from your 90th birthday when that was taken.

It must have been a bitter sweet day for you, a happy occasion yet a reminder that Helen wasn't there to see her son Stephen marrying Leagh. I know that I spent most of the ceremony in uncontrollable tears, like the loss of Helen six years earlier suddenly hit me like a tidal wave. I can only imagine how hard it was for you. I lost a sister but you lost a daughter. Likewise with Ronan. I lost a brother. You lost a son. I know now that you are reunited with both, along with Daddy who no doubt is clicking his heels in heavenly glee to have his Maura back alongside him. I know you're happy too. I could see it on your face when you were laid out. It was a look of pure serenity.

Speaking of Ronan, because he was 8 years older than I, it was like he was the big brother of another generation. However, I have these great little vignettes in my head going back to one Christmas when you were making the Christmas cake while Ronan, Ciaran and I hovered like vultures to sneak a little icing or marzipan, or to pounce on the floor like a royal scrum when you'd "accidentally on purpose" let some of the multi-colored, edible cake decorations fall. You'd think we had never seen a piece of cake before! However, there was something special about your Christmas cake, passed down from your mother before you. It was light, moist and delicious, with or without butter. Maybe I'll make it again this year, like I did in 2013 with your guidance. You'll be glad to know I kept your wooden spoon and the baking bowl, which Ciaran is kindly minding for me at the cottage in Killarney. Isn't it great about Ciaran's retirement in Killarney, the place of our childhood holidays and Daddy's home town. Great memories and such a special place. Who knows I might end up there for Christmas this year.

I know you were really never one for Christmas. It stirred up emotions and sadness, as it does for so many people. We're all under pressure to be happy and drink up, when inside our hearts are aching. I find myself wondering how I'll get through this Christmas, the first one without you. I think it will be especially difficult for Anne as you always went to Anne and David for Christmas Day. There will be a big void at that dinner table without you.

Indeed, there was a big void this past summer when I went home and you weren't there. I slept in your bed which I thought would be strange but actually it was very comforting. However, there were so many times I just wanted to get into Ciaran's car and drive over to visit you at Holy Family Residence. You were truly content in that nursing home and so well cared for. You had great company with staff, residents and daily visitors, or alone time in your Room 101 with a good book or the TV. You loved watching Dáithí and Maura's *Today Show* in the afternoons, or a good Nature programme, and you'd sit up in bed with a nightcap in hand, generously poured by Sister Gertrude.

Those sisters gave you the most beautiful funeral. Along with Anne, Ciaran and myself, they all gathered in the foyer to welcome you home when you arrived in the hearse. We picked a beautiful rich mahogany coffin at Fanagans who had you beautifully turned out in your white suit, fuchsia pink and purple scarf, all cradled in white satin with lace trim. You were still regal. When they settled you into the room upstairs, double doors open wide and wall to wall window, the morning sun came up over the garden outside like a divine presence. You always loved the sunshine. God was welcoming you home.

The day of your funeral, the Holy Family Residence chapel was packed to capacity. Your wishes were granted to have Catherine and Patricia, our first cousins, doing the music, including your special wish, "The Rose" and "The Wind Beneath My Wings". Your departure from the Residence was one that I will never forget. The family, including Anne, David, Ciaran, Auntie Pat and I, sat into the funeral car to follow you. Between your car and ours, the nuns and staff walked in procession behind you, saying the rosary along the winding driveway. As the hearse stopped before exiting the gate, they all stood with reverence to the side and waved you off in unison. It was like a scene from a film, a most beautiful send off. As my friend Marion said, "there was a wonderful sense of completion" about your life. Only three weeks from your 97th birthday, you passed peacefully on Good Friday morning, a very special and symbolic day to go. Though heartbroken to lose you, I remind myself that it was a blessing you were taken quickly after your stroke rather than have you suffer with no quality of life.

You died in dignity as you had lived, a most elegant woman, a devoted mother and a Lady to your perfectly manicured fingertips. I'm eternally grateful for the selfless love and generosity you showed me, the myriad of memories to comfort me and so proud to be your daughter. I will carry on your graceful legacy as best I can and live well in your honour. I love you dearly, miss you terribly but know you are at peace. To quote one of your favourite writers, Helen Steiner Rice "Your mother is still with you — She never left your side. She still is close about you — her spirit is your guide."

Till we meet again at the heavenly gates, Codladh Samh, a mhathair.

Love always,
Olivia

OLIVIA TRACEY
Olivia Tracey became Miss Ireland in 1983 and went on to become the only Irish contestant to ever become a finalist in the Miss Universe contest. Now living in LA, she is an actress and producer, known for *The Island* (2005), *Lucky You* (2007) and *Gilmore Girls* (2000). She regularly returns to Ireland to visit family and undertake modeling assignments, and she is a popular guest on *The Late Late Show*.

> *You both taught me everything I know, except how to live without you.*

Simon Young writes to Carmel and Tom Young

Dear Mom and Dad

I've been asked to drop you a special letter and it's tougher than I thought it would be. Like some of the fairy cakes Mom made you bake, Dad, hand grenades!

Missing you seems so inadequate. It's a lot deeper than that as 'Love Never Goes Away.' I miss you greatly and respectfully as you sure did your best for us. We all just knew that we came first. You never once raised your voice to us, never mind your hand, but you explained everything and where we had gone wrong. You worked very hard Dad as a typewriter mechanic, and you were always doing a nixer on the kitchen table after tea (3 courses!) to make sure that we had a so cosy caravan summer holiday.

I just don't know how you did it Mom. Working in Lipton's all of your life gave you a great knowledge of spices and tastes. I used to watch you make all sorts of cakes in our tiny kitchen in Finglas, and fresh brown or soda bread every single morning. Finglas was a bit of a concrete jungle at the time. I think that's why you sent us to a private school, St. Vincent's in Glasnevin.

But as time passed we gathered the best of neighbours. How we all laughed belly tears one summer. Dad had just planted a lovely tree in the front garden, remember Dad? You then placed your arms around Glenn and I and said, 'Do you see that tree lads, well that's going to be there long after we're all gone. The next morning it was gone! Oh, such happy times.

You both always explained everything to us so well, and I used to listen to all that came from my brilliant parents. You were an amazing Mom & Dad and we wanted for nothing. Mom, you were well known as the 'Lady Of Ratoath Avenue' and would do anything for anyone, and even leave yourself short. God, how I truly miss you both. I pray every night that you have found each other again up in the stars and are so happy again. Mom was lost when you passed away Dad and she never really got over it. I was delighted that her last words to me were 'You always made me laugh.'

Well, in my eyes you're together again. Missing you both, the pain is so great because the love was so deep.

You both taught me everything I know, except how to live without you.

Your loving son,
Simon

SIMON YOUNG
Simon Young is a former Irish radio and television presenter, who at one stage in the 1990s had the whole country using his catch phrase, "Ger owa dat garden"!

He was a presenter on RTÉ 2FM on *The Beatbox* and the *Weekend Breakfast Show*, and also made regular appearances on television on *Dempsey's Den*, presented by his friend and colleague Ian Dempsey. He retired from broadcasting in 2002, and has spoken out about mental health issues.

I can't believe I'm writing about you in the past tense – here come the tears again, dammit – but you would have embraced them too: 'It's all right to cry' – and you would probably be crying along with me, which you frequently did.

Deirdre Purcell writes to Patricia Byrne

Dear Patricia

You are not dead, are you?

You couldn't be — not you, you whose life embraced, in the literal meaning of the word, the planet that in your latter years of "retirement" (hah!) you explored with Frank — and of course one of your multiplicity of 'gangs', the furthest reaches of the earth, the more exotic the better.

Your open arms and redoubtable spirit took in not just your ever-widening family, to include in-laws, their in-laws, their children's children and in-laws, your multiple and overlapping circles of friends who included me, but your work on behalf of others that became crucial in so many people's lives.

So despite the bottomless well of tears I have shed before and since you left me on August 16 2017, you are not dead and shall be alive to me until I join you, wherever that is.

We had so many discussions about that wherever. You were reluctant to let go of the notion that you would again meet your beloved parents, Tom and Stella, "somewhere"; you were looking forward to joining them, you said, when my parents, Bill and Maureen, would throw you a massive party to celebrate your arrival amongst them again. And all present watched for Stella to take off her earrings so the real party — i.e. the singing and dancing — could start on Maureen's nearly-new carpet while Bill distributed the stout and small Jemmies from the sideboard.

'But what do you think?' you would ask, then listen carefully to my crackpot, ragbag theories about what actually happens after we die. Our bodies, like everything in our universe, being composed of matter — molecules and atoms — and is thereby eternal and infinite, like heaven and maybe our universe, one of many — perhaps. 'Stardust,' I told you, 'we were all created from stardust, and our existence as human beings are transitional until our personal matter transmogrifies after death. It recreates itself, perhaps over millennia, into different forms and maybe it evolves, eventually, again into human form.

'But our souls and spirits, what happens to them?'

'They disperse, survive, contribute, become part of the evolution but in a way that right now we can't see.'

'But if Mammy and Daddy are transmogrifying too, how will I know them when I meet them? And suppose we don't get to be human at the same time?'

'You won't recognise them, probably,' I would say airily, but then, seeing your frown as you tried to work this out and pretending a confidence I didn't feel, I'd add something along the lines of: 'You could sense that something or someone you come across is familiar; you could be drawn unexpectedly to a person or object for a reason you can't explain.'

'So Frank could be some old great-great-great granny of mine, then? Or a milk jug she owned once?'

We'd both dissolve. You had a fabulous giggle, Patricia. It was irresistible.

But although we could never see eye-to-eye on this issue, the big thing was, you were open in every way — to new friendships, new causes, new experiences; your loyalty to me was without parallel; no matter what I went through, good or bad, you embraced me and therefore it. You rejoiced with me, mourned with me, defended me, supported me when I struggled, gave out trenchantly about people you decided had done me wrong.

I can't believe I'm writing about you in the past tense — here come the tears again, dammit — but you would have embraced them too: 'It's all right to cry' — and you would probably be crying along with me, which you frequently did.

You see the thing is, you were so vibrantly alive through three sets of cancer treatments, so strongly and resolutely optimistic about outcomes, so altruistic throughout in trying to ensure you did not forget the vicissitudes of my life, it's impossible for me to believe that you're not there any more.

In the last phase of your illness, like the petals of a sunflower closing around its heart at dusk, your immediate, wonderful family folded protectively around your bed in the Mater but with just hours to go, Frank offered me a chance to say goodbye...

It was the most difficult meeting of my life, Patricia, but you were being palliatively cared for at that stage so I truly hope it wasn't as difficult for you. You smiled at me while I uttered my usual inanities while stroking your hair and your arm. I asked if you were peaceful, your response was typical: 'I feel very lucky. Very, very lucky.'

And you were. With your family. With your job right up to the end as a social worker in the inner city; with your friends as confidante-in chief. I hope you knew this and although from my perspective you did not see the extent of the crowds who turned up over the two days of your obsequies — by some estimates up to a thousand — from yours you did see us all and you were aghast. I can hear you: 'What are they all doing here? Tell them to go home for God's sake — '

I knew you for far more years than I knew my mother, my father, my brother, my sons or husbands; we were friends for more than seven decades. We were walked out in our prams by best friends, our mothers, Maureen and Stella; I remember your fourth birthday party when you, unspeakably, got a blue silk "bell dress" i.e. its hem jingling all around with tiny bells, sent to you in a parcel from America; we competed with each other as to who'd still have chips left in Cunningham's chipshop in Tramore when we were nine; we were taught to swim by your father, Tom; we accepted without question that your Stella and my Maureen kept small bottles of sherry under the sink to go with the cups of tea in the afternoon; far more advanced than I although you were a year younger, you taught me how to kiss, you picked up the pieces after my first marriage collapsed, you welcomed my second with open arms; you helped me clear out the house in Ballymun after Maureen died, you brought me soggy tomato sandwiches when I was hospitalised, you egged me on in Peacock's clothes shop in the Omni Centre, you endorsed my salt habit when we dined in Eddie Rockets, snored gently beside me during movies, became indignant on my behalf if someone hurt me.

We knew each other inside out, we could use verbal shorthand from that long knowing; in many ways, you were the better part of me, Patricia. What will I do without you?

But I can now hear you again: 'Shut up! You'll survive.

You always do. You're a born survivor, because you've had to be.'

So of course I'll go on. It'll be hard but I know I've lost only your physical presence and that I won't lose your spirit or your voice.

You loved gardens and nature. I wanted to tell you, but can't now, that the 250-year old Beech tree outside my window is shedding its leaves. It will be the last of the trees around here to come back into leaf but it always does. It's one of the great events of my year, every year — firstly a swelling here and there, then a greenish bloom of buds, and then, maybe after a heavy sun shower, all those buds, hundreds of thousands of them, open to the light and my tree, in crown and cape of fresh new green, celebrates its survival of another winter, another set of storms and rains.

You won't come visibly to me any more but you'll be there. You will, Patricia. Thank you.

Deirdre

DEIRDRE PURCELL

Deirdre Purcell is from Dublin. She had an eclectic set of careers, including acting at the Abbey Theatre, before she became a journalist and writer, winning awards for her work on the *Sunday Tribune*. She has published thirteen critically acclaimed novels, most recently *Pearl* and *The Winter Gathering*, all of which have been bestsellers in Ireland. She adapted *Falling for a Dancer* into a poplar four-part television mini-series, while *Love Like Hate Adore* was shortlisted for the Orange Prize.

I will go on our adventures, I will go to the weddings, I will love and hug our children, and in time our grandchildren, for the both of us. And when I see you again I will be old and tired for having lived a life for the both of us.

Bernard Lucas writes to Caitriona Lucas

Dear Caitriona

A lot has changed since you went to sleep. I have asked myself lots of questions. Why did it have to happen to you? Why didn't I go with you that day? Maybe I could have saved you. I have asked God why did he let it happen? Is there a God?

I think often of all the things you are going to miss out on, the kids' weddings, grandchildren, your beloved nieces and nephews growing up, Christmases, birthday parties. All the places we wanted to travel to and the adventures we wanted to go on. But life threw us a curved ball. People say give it time. But what does time mean? I knew and loved you for 24 years. Is that what they mean?

I remember the first time I met you. You were 16 and wearing your leather jacket and your infectious smile and I was hooked. Is that the time? Is it the time I will have to spend without you? I guess it's the latter they mean, and in some ways I am beginning to realise what they mean.

We were in pieces after the accident, but it has been 15 months and 19 days as I write. The pieces are still there, but maybe not as small.

Every now and then I get caught out. I walk around the back of the house and see your jeep and for a split second I think, Caitriona is home, and my heart jumps with joy. Or I wake up in the middle of the night and think it has all been a nightmare, and I turn over and you're not there. But now instead of tears [they still happen sometimes] I have memories. Beautiful, happy, fun memories. I am happy for lots of things in my life but I am happiest for having met and shared part of my life with you. I am the person I am because of who you were.

You would not want us to give up or live in sadness. You would want us to live our lives to the full. You were an inspiration to a lot of people and you continue to inspire me. Your courage and commitment to helping others was astounding, and I draw strength from that every day. I watch our beautiful daughter miss you every day, but like you she is strong and brave. She has started college, passed her driving test, and has a boyfriend. You would like him. You would be so proud of her. Our son — the strong silent one in the early stages — he held everything together. He misses you so much but I see him take inspiration from the way you lived your life, and he is doing well. He just got a promotion at work again, you would be so proud.

I am beginning to see time is a healer, so I will try and live my life to the full. I will go on our adventures, I will go to the weddings, I will love and hug our children and in time our grandchildren, for the both of us. And when I see you again I will be old and tired for having lived a life for the both of us.

Forever yours
Bernard xx

BERNARD LUCAS
Bernard Lucas is a Coast Guard volunteer in Doolin, Co Clare, since 2002. He and his wife, Caitriona, who joined the service in 2004, turned their love of the

outdoors — boats, water, climbing — into a dedicated commitment to giving back to their community. Caitriona was the first volunteer at an incident in September 2016, when she lost her life in a boat accident. Bernard has continued taking part in regular rescue missions, and says Caitriona's memory sustains him, and continues to inspire him and their children Ben and Emma.

The love we feel for you is unrelenting, we will live our lives to honour the two most beautiful brave souls this world has ever seen. We strive to make you proud of us each and every day.

Tony and Mary Heffernan write to Saoirse and Liam Heffernan

Dear Saoirse and Liam

We are writing this letter to let you know that despite all that has happened Mommy and Daddy are doing ok. We miss you so very much each and every moment of each and every day.

It feels so strange writing this letter. It feels so wrong. Wrong in the sense that you are in heaven, our beautiful courageous babies, gone and never coming home to us again. Yet we are still here, living our lives as best we can. But promises were made and we vowed to you that we would try our very best to make Ireland a better place for sick children. So the show must go on, because if there is one thing that we are not prepared to do, it is to break that promise.

We often sit in the silence of home and remember all the things you got up to when you were here. We have so many laugh out loud moments, like the time Saoirse that you welded your mouth shut with toffee. Or the time you locked yourself into Granda's car. We panicked — you laughed your head off. Or Liamo when you'd beg for just one more bedtime story, even though we would have already read fifteen. Or when you'd wake at three in the morning and tell us you were off for a bath.

Going back to Inch beach was a favourite of all four of us, and of course the dogs. The hours we spent there making sand castles, climbing the sand dunes, running into the water, having picnics and just totally enjoying life. When you went to heaven Saoirse it was the main place that gave Liamo comfort, and now that you are both in heaven it's the go-to place for us when things get on top of us. We feel a great connection to you there, all the wonderful memories come flooding back, and life seems bearable again. We took so much for granted.

Looking back it is still so hard to comprehend what has happened. One minute we were a happy family of four, getting on with life, and the next thing we knew we were thrown into a black hole with absolutely no way out. In a very short space of time we had to face the unfaceable and bear the unbearable. The single and only thing that sustained us throughout that horror was the two of you. How could your Mommy and Daddy crumble when you showed a bravery far beyond your years; when you continued to smile despite the horrors that were being visited upon you. We were, and still are, simply in awe of you.

Battens Disease is a monster that comes with a cruelty that is way beyond our understanding. Battens Disease took so much from you, and eventually took your lives, but it never took your fighting spirit, your ability to love and be loved, your dignity. Its brutal claws were always on the prowl. God knows it tried hard but you were not for turning. Throughout this period the two of you taught us so much, we cannot begin to tell you how proud we are of you. There simply are no words, it's beyond words.

So now kiddos it's time for Mommy and Daddy to say goodbye to the life we planned, so that we can embrace the life that God has asked us to live. We will always and forever carry you both with us, and we know that each day would be an impossible task were it not for the love and strength you showed us in the short time we had the privilege to have you here with us. Your light is the light that will guide us for our remaining days.

The love we feel for you is unrelenting. We will live our lives to honour the two most beautiful, brave souls this world has ever seen. We strive to make you proud of us each and every day. We know that time is the greatest currency we have, so we intend to spend it wisely.

Sleep tight now our beauties. Saoirse we are sending you fondies and a hug, hug, hug. And to you Liamo a big hug, a big kiss and a big squeeze!

Love ye lots like jelly tots.............xxxxxxx
Forever and always until we meet again
Mommy and Daddy

TONY AND MARY HEFFERNAN
Tony and Mary Heffernan are the founders of the Bumbleance ambulance service for children with rare diseases. They have won the Irish Mirror Pride of Ireland award in recognition of their work.

They set up the charity the Saoirse Foundation — Bee For Battens — after their daughter Saoirse was diagnosed with Batten's Disease. Their second child Liam was diagnosed with Batten's shortly afterwards. Saoirse passed away when she was five and Liam when he reached the same age.

The couple have helped dozens of other families whose children have rare illnesses, and are raising €4.5million for a new respite centre in Co Kerry — Liam's Lodge.

Things are different now, though. Life moves faster, yet progress seems slower. I would give anything for a day in the hayfield again, sun shining and a can of sugary tea in the field.

Mairead McGuinness writes to Mella and John McGuinness

Dear Mella and John

It seems strange to be writing to you for the first and probably the last time.

Letters weren't necessary because you always spoke to us on the phone, religiously, daily.

It's been a long time since we were together — all 10 of us — you both and the gang of eight children. It must be... yes... I remember now, at Paddy's funeral, some 20 years ago. He was the 11th member of the family, our unmarried uncle who farmed with us and lived nearby but spent all his time with us. Can you remember his devotion to polishing our school shoes — eight pairs of Clarkes' best in black or brown, with laces and buckles? It remains one of the most vivid pictures I have in my mind. He took great pride in shining them.

There is so much to tell you about how your grandchildren are and what we're all up to now.

I know you might be sad that our house at 'The Glebe', Ardee, is no longer home to any McGuinnesses. But it is a home still and a good one. We got together a few months after you, Mella, passed away in 2013 to share the things that mattered most to you. It was a day filled with sadness, papered over with laughter, as we jollied ourselves along sorting the contents and looking at old photographs and random bits of stuff bought on school excursions as gifts for you, which you always treasured. I wonder did you know then that they would also mean so much to us, too, many years later when you would no longer be around. I suspect you did.

And a big thank you, by the way, for the bundles you saved for each of us — a compilation of school reports, newspaper cuttings and in my case the hand written cards for my speech at the official opening of Ardee Community School in 1975! I also have some other pieces of your lives together, including mementos of your many travels abroad to Russia, most of Europe, the US and Canada. In the photographs you look happy together, which of course you were — because you were always together! You, mother were the great dreamer and schemer and Daddy the very willing executor of your grand plans... which always worked out really well.

I don't know how you, Daddy, put up with mother's constant desire to change the house — knocking down walls and building extensions. Maybe it was because our original home was burned down completely in a fire in 1960 and you rebuilt it quickly that you were so keen to re-shape the bungalow over the years. I'm in awe at how you managed to keep going after losing so much in that fire, but you always said that as no one was badly hurt then everything else could be replaced.

Are there any bikes where you are Daddy? Like the racer you used to cycle from the farmyard to the house? And Mammy do you remember how he would cycle to the big kitchen window and look in with his loving eyes and blow kisses? Not to mention you both waltzing around the kitchen on occasion.

There were tough times too, when one by one we all left home. I'm only now realising, as my own gang move on, how awful that must have been to see our close-knit family unravel.

I used to cry in the back of the car when we were leaving home as I started my studies in UCD in 1976. I'm sure you cried too when some of us not only left home but left the country too.

You probably feared for us as we headed off into the world, just as we fear now for our own children.

The twins are 23 now. Do you remember when Gay Byrne announced their arrival on his radio programme? You were thrilled — so was I! You were a great help when they were little. In fact you were amazing with all the grand-children, making delicious dinners and getting them to eat by playing games with spoons swooping into tiny mouths like aeroplanes landing!

In the cow versus chicken race, the chicken won! And while cows are no longer being milked at home, there is another generation of McGuinnesses on the farm.

It's a pity you missed my move into politics Daddy. Mother saw me through several elections — canvassing in her own way and fretting when things got tough.

We ate the last of the victoria plums yesterday. You both loved plums. Every autumn I stand under our plum trees and salute you both and recall times past when we would gorge on juicy plums fresh from the trees. And we still manage to make damson jam too. Things are different now though. Life moves faster, yet progress seems slower. I would give anything for a day in the hayfield again, sun shining and a can of sugary tea in the field.

I try not to think of the final days when ill health hit both of you. But I will never forget the last time you were at home together in your bed, both sick and sad. I brought you mother to the hospital knowing that you would probably never be in that place called home together again, ever.

I still wonder did we do enough to ease your pain.

Nothing prepares you for the grief of losing your parents which you, in your time, went through too.

Your favourite film was *The Lion King*, the cartoon movie we watched with the children, singing along to the song *The Circle of Life*... with its message about life, parting, moving on and remembering who you are and where you come from.

Great movie, powerful song. Great memories.

Love always,

Mairead

MAIREAD McGUINNESS

Mairead McGuinness is first vice-president of the European Parliament. She represents 15 counties in the Midlands North West Constituency. Born on a farm near Ardee, Co Louth, she now lives on a farm in Co Meath with her husband, Tom Duff, and four children. The McGuinness family were market gardeners in the past, growing vegetables and fruit and supplying the local market. Mairead is one of eight children born to John and Mella (née McMahon) in June 1959. They experienced the hardships of farming pre-EU membership and the changes which joining the then EEC brought. Hard working, family focused, their lives reflect the realities of many farming families of those times.

... that pain gradually turned to an ache, which eventually turned into guilt - for words left unsaid, things undone and the longing to be able to spend time and talk with you both one last time.

Tommy Fleming writes to Annie and Paddy Fleming

Dear Mam and Dad

How're things? It's been a while since we spoke properly, so I've decided to put pen to paper and let you know everything that's happened since we last saw you.

The void that you both left in our lives after you passed away on March 30th 2012 was enormous. Nothing could have prepared me for the heart wrenching pain of your loss. It's been a long road to finally be able to smile when I'm transported to a memory of you both, be it the smell of geraniums or the sight of a perfectly manicured vegetable garden. I now feel these are a message from you to say you're doing great, and that we should live our lives to the fullest and embrace every opportunity that's presented to us.

It was so hard to comprehend or even believe that you were both gone in the weeks after your funeral/funerals? (I never know if its singular or plural) so I'll go with funeral as I always saw you both as one. It took a lot of soul searching to try and understand my grief, and when I couldn't understand it I tried to tell myself that you were both on a very long holiday in a place with everything you loved around you — a lush vegetable garden for you Dad, chickens for you Mam. I wanted to believe that wherever you were, you were both happy to be there, and that you were watching out for us all and sending signs every now and then that you were OK. You will be pleased to know we have a resident robin who visits us daily, and I know is you dropping in to say hello.

I won't pretend to you that life was OK after you passed, because it wasn't. I missed you both so much that I can honestly say I physically had a pain in my heart. But that pain gradually turned to an ache, which eventually turned into guilt for words left unsaid, things undone, and the longing to be able to talk with you both one last time. I knew this was an impossible wish, but as you both know too well, I'm a dreamer.

My life has been great thus far with my family and career. There isn't a capital city around the world I haven't touched down in. But I guess you know that already because you both keep me safe on every journey and adventure I go on. When I arrive in a destination I always wish I could call you to let you know what's happening, as I always did following Mam's rule of "Ring when you land". In the first few months I would forget, and for a split second the awful empty realization that you were gone would hit me with a lonely sadness I can never explain. But that too subsided somewhat, and I now talk quite frequently to both of you. I guess its my idea of praying. Ha!

You always tried to teach me not to have regrets in life, but I cannot help the regret I feel that you haven't been there for all the rewards I have had in my life. These are rewards that you helped and encouraged me to achieve, and when I would doubt everything I was doing or believed in, you helped me believe again. I know you will continue to guide me, as you continue to guide us all on whatever road we choose to take, and I can never thank you both enough for all the love and support you gave us. You let us "be all we could be", and so until we meet again.

We miss you terribly.

Love always.
Tommy (Or Tom as you affectionately called me)

TOMMY FLEMING

Tommy Fleming is described as the Voice of Ireland and is one of the finest singers of his generation. After 25 years honing his craft, Tommy is now taking his place at the forefront of popular music across the globe. While his music may be difficult to classify, fans use such words as deeply emotional, romantic and sincere to describe the feelings it evokes. One reviewer has described his music as falling into a genre of Symphonic Pop that still awaits a name.

Tommy is only now coming to terms with the shocking loss of both his parents on the same day, five years ago. While both had been ill for some time, neither Tommy nor his siblings ever imagined that their beloved Mam and Dad would leave within hours of each other.

Sometimes our bodies shake and our hearts beat desperately. Other times we can feel the calm which comes as an ocean breeze that refreshes our faces.

Tom and Tatiana Fay write to Lorena Fay

Dear Lorena

It hasn't been easy living without you. The challenges we face daily along with a lack of support from the ones we expected most; societal attitudes with no understanding also being an issue. It has become quite tiresome listening to people telling us what we should or shouldn't be doing, how we should be acting and how we should be feeling. As it has been over a year since you left, it is expected that we just move on. What people can't understand is that you didn't go, and you will never go, from our thoughts and our hearts.

You are an essential part of us, and even if we cannot see or touch you we still feel and connect with you every day, and this feeling is becoming more intense as the days go by.

All the lovely moments that we spent together will be stuck in our hearts forever. Thank you for the hugs, kisses, cuddles and jokes. We will keep also the hard moments in our thoughts, to constantly remind us that life is so short and precious. We've learned this through the most traumatic and tragic circumstances.

You were a such a small baby who has had a huge impact on our lives. You had a short life but you are still alive in our hearts. We are grateful and thankful that you chose us to be your parents, and we thank you for the gifts that you have given us whilst spending time on this Earth school.

We think of you so many times a day, Lorena. Sometimes

our bodies shake and our hearts beat desperately. Other times we feel calm as an ocean breeze refreshing our faces. Then we have days where the tears roll down our faces and we can't breathe. The dark days are an incredible torture. We never know when they will come, but they come taking away all the peace and the hope we are trying to build up. Those days are a nightmare and all the questions — why me, why us, why is life so unfair pop into our heads. But some days we can feel the softness of your skin, the sweetness of your smell and it calms our hours and refreshes our souls.

You are part of us. The scar on Mammy's belly is you on her body. The goodness in our attitudes is you in our actions. The reason to keep going and continuing with life is you filling us with your love.

We used to say that you "jumped the wall" before us, but we will meet again some day and we will never more be apart.

We love you, sweetheart! With all our hearts and souls. Forever and ever!

Mamãe and Papai
xxxxxxxxxxx

TOM AND TATIANA FAY
Tatiana and Tomas met in 2014. She is Brazilian and he is Irish. On their first trip to Brazil the following year they found out they were expecting their first child Lorena.

Lorena was born 31st July 2016 and she had Downs Syndrome, which was unknown by her parents right

up until when she was born. She also had the worst transient form of Leukemia known as TAM (Transient Abnormal Myelopoiesis). Both parents fell in love with their beautiful little daughter Lorena and tried everything to save her but unfortunately her health deteriorated and she passed away on 19th of August 2016. Both parents are heartbroken, however they have openly accepted the gifts their daughter has given both of them, the main gift being love. Their mission is to help others who cannot cope so well and try to educate society in dealing with bereaved parents and helping parents who have lost a child.

Grief is everyday survival. It is tears at least once a day, a solitary sadness that never leaves. You wear it like an invisible coat. No one else can see it but you know you are wearing it.

Josepha Madigan writes to Edwina Madigan Ion

Dear Edwina (aka Cooch)

Do you remember your Bosco pyjama and slipper set when you were small? How you loved them! You wouldn't wear anything else to bed for quite a while. The cute squished up face of your Cabbage patch doll went everywhere with you too. It was called 'Premie' because it was a premature cabbage patch doll with its own birth certificate. I know, mad isn't it? In the early eighties no one batted an eyelid. Do you remember how we used to sing "You take the high road and I'll take the low road and I'll be in Scotland before you" at bedtime? I don't know which is funnier, the fact that you subsequently married a Scot (you can blame me for all that brainwashing) or that you endured my out-of-tune singing. It was fun.

I am in love with you right from the start. Visiting the Stella Maris Nursing Home, you look up at me with wise eyes, like a small owl, swaddled in white. Your hair is jet black. You have long fingers and toes. You might be small but our home becomes your barn. We are all charmed and besotted by you in equal measure. I am eleven and you are my fourth and youngest sister. You are the baby of the family. I cherish the memories. Jagged little videos that play out in my mind's eye: stuffing your plump body into a purple babygro and all the fasteners popping one by one; rocking you to sleep in the wooden swingcot, beige carpet hairs over my school uniform as I creep out the door on my belly; putting on your woolly hat, mittens on a string and scarf before we go to the garden to make mud pies; eating strawberry flavour Angel delight together and making Soda streams; letting you change in the back of the car into more suitable attire for Wes as you got older (sorry Mum!). You see Cooch, nothing lasts forever. Not Bosco, the Cabbage Patch doll, the Stella Maris or even you. But your spirit does. Of that I am sure.

Today is your funeral. We throw sunflowers, one by one, into the deep clay abyss of your grave. Your coffin lies on top of Dad's coffin, both of you victims of cancer's brutal and prolific appetite for destruction. Our brother and your three other older sisters mourn your loss acutely. I don't own their grief nor is it mine to share. I can only speak to my own. Our mother is as strong as an oak tree but my heart bleeds for her. For your husband, I wish him nothing but warmth, happiness and love for the rest of his days. We all navigate tentatively through unchartered waters. We cry, we reminisce, but mostly we grieve. Alone but together. Grief is selfish and lonely. No one can do it for you nor take it away from you. Grief is every day survival. It is tears at least once a day, a solitary sadness that never leaves. You wear it like an invisible coat. No one else can see it but you know you are wearing it. No matter where you go or what you do, the coat stays on.

I sit in the yacht club for the funeral lunch. I don't remember what we eat or if we eat anything at all. Do they even serve food? I don't recall the conversations either. Maybe we just sit there in silence like mute companions. I peer out the bay window. My eyes flicker past the boats at the harbour onto the pier. I observe the couples, friends, solo walkers, dog walkers, fitness freaks and the disenfranchised. How can they just walk along as if nothing has changed? Do they not know my youngest sister is dead? That today her bodily remains are left behind with our father deep in the dark soil? How can they be impervious to our torment? I watch as a lady laughs. She throws her head back and guffaws loudly. I don't understand the language she speaks. I am underwater now, suffocated in tight bubble wrap. It's a self-imposed armour, a cruel knee-jerk reaction to grief. In one week it is your first anniversary. Slowly the swollen bubbles burst open one by one. Each small explosion jolts me clumsily into a reality I don't want to be in. But I am. We all are. The water seeps in through the tiny holes and I dare to breathe. We go on. Like newborns we are raw and sensitive.

The day after your funeral I find myself alone on Dún Laoghaire pier. I don't even bring the dog. She implores me with her doe-eyes but I leave her behind. I need to be alone. I look out at the sparkly stillness of the water. I feel instantly like hurtling myself off the pier down into the cover of the deep blue blanket of sea. I want the water to stifle the sharp sting emanating from the emotions within me, to somehow annihilate the pain. I want all and each one of the difficult feelings within me obliterated. I shudder and pull my jacket collar up. It's cooler here. I put on my headphones. I pace up and down the concrete slabs as if my life depends upon it. As if I can walk the torture away. But I can't. I never take my eyes off the twinkling surface, the picturesque vista of bobbing yachts a balm to sore, jaded eyes. Eyes that wish they avoided witnessing your slow demise, the unfurling of your beautiful spirit from its beautiful body. We are left bereft.

At times when I stare out to the horizon, Dad sidles in beside you, hugging you, holding you close. Cooch, he calls you. Pops you call him. I sense your smiles for real, your arms around each other's waists, dancing together to Ring-a-Rosie, happy and carefree. Sia's *Chandelier* comes up on my iPhone shuffle. The tears fall hard behind my sunglasses (yes I know it's not sunny). My voice strains to sing every word, the wind catching my voice and carrying it muffled and distorted across the bay. (Yes, Cooch, this time I have an excuse to be out-of-tune). I lose tissues and my mind as I walk and walk. I walk the pier every evening for three weeks. Then I stop. I feel close to you at the pier. I know that's because I am. It's where you find it easiest to slip deftly through the slight tear in the veil between your world and ours. It's where I can hear you whisper, feel your sweet presence and connect with your gentle spirit. I think it's where you are most at home. Even if it's not, it gives me some comfort.

Like Sia, Cooch, I promise you I will swing from the chandeliers (not like that you bold thing!) You know what I mean. I will endeavour to extract every ounce out of every day. I promise I will do my best to honour life itself, the sacred gift that it is. I promise to live, as best I can, a self-actualised life. I know you would want that. Sia says to live each day as if tomorrow doesn't exist. I promise I will try. When I am scared, afraid or plain terrified, I think of you. Time is running out. I know you would not want me to waste a single second of it. Life can change abruptly. It can change in an instant. The time is now. I think of you and Dad. I thank God to have known you both, to have been inspired by you both, to have loved and been loved by you both.

I miss you.
Josepha

JOSEPHA MADIGAN

After practising as a solicitor for two decades, Josepha Madigan was elected as the Fine Gael TD for Dublin Rathdown in 2016, and became Minister for Culture Heritage and the Gaeltacht in November 2017. She is the author of *ADR in Ireland, A Handbook for Family Lawyers and their Clients* (Jordan publishing, 2012). She is married to Finbarr and they have two sons and a dog.

"It was a difficult decision to agree to write this letter, but the hospice and its ancillary services are a lifeline to so many. I know that Dad and Edwina would want me to help. There is equally no shame in grief. As Marianne Williamson says it is a process not an event best served by surrendering to it completely."

You loved and lived for us, your sons, but we knew at any moment we could be sold into slavery for a single hour of Luciano Pavarotti live. You would travel anywhere to hear him sing.

Gavin Duffy writes to Ann Duffy

Dear Mam

Though your death was expected, it came as a huge shock to us all. You, who were a woman of such tenacity, fortitude and resilience, had finally left us. All the people who came to sympathise with us said you were a 'Lady'. Certainly you were from a different era, born in hard times 1926.

You and your brothers and sisters — Edward, the generous one; Johnny the boxing champion; Bill, the war hero, a miraculous survivor of the atom bomb in Nagasaski; George, the entrepreneur; Desmond, the little brother with the big heart; Pearl the great educator, and May the beauty queen — all had to 'take the boat', forced to emigrate. But you were all of strong stock, and for you emigration was no penance but an opportunity. You prospered. Your brothers used to joke that they powered London. George, the boss at Battersea Power Station, gave many a son of the West a start.

You returned home to Ireland after the Second World War and in 1952 married the love of your life, Edward Duffy. You had given us clear instructions that your ashes were to be placed alongside his in Glasnevin Cemetery. Your rollercoaster romance had seen you separate in the seventies and reunite in the nineties, and now you are joined for eternity. How often did we hear you say, 'stay the course'.

You saw so many things in your life. Rural electrification in the West, bigotry in Belfast, Luftwaffe bombing in London, the birth of Irish television, Mayo winning the Sam, lunar landings, central heating, the fax machine, and the mobile phone, perhaps your favourite. You were an early adapter and adopter, but refused to advance beyond your trusty Nokia. You used it as a magic wand to issue instructions, edicts and orders to your sons. And when the message was in CAPS it meant, do it now!

You loved and lived for us, your sons, but we knew at any moment we could be sold into slavery for a single hour of Luciano Pavarotti live. You would travel anywhere to hear him sing. Your love of opera and classical music was inherited from your own mother, while the card playing came from your mother-in-law, Mom Duffy. The move from being a young card shark at the game of 25 to respectable Bridge devotee was life changing. Not only could you play Bridge all night but you were well capable of talking about those hands, in excruciating detail, all the following day. The family learned that Bridge is not a game of cards but a fraternity, and all the visits in your last months from the Bridge gang were cherished by you.

The wider family will remember a mother, grandmother, great grandmother, aunty and matriarch for two things especially — style and travel. You didn't just follow fashion,you set it. Days at Punchestown and the old Phoenix Park race course, and nights in Clontarf Castle were your favourites.

Your grandchildren, now of back-packing age, have a lot of travelling to do to catch up. You trekked the Amazon Jungle, safaried in Africa, brazened the bazaars of the Indian continent, shopped New York, partied in New Orleans, climbed the great Wall, wailed at the wall and railed against Trump's wall.

You were always politically aware, and an advocate for

gender equality. Though true to your faith you were most critical of religiosity, and nieces and daughters-in-law would be told about the lunacy of women of your time being 'churched' after child birth.

Nor were you pleased with the changes, for the worse you believed, over the years, to your beloved West Street in Drogheda. Many of Drogheda's business community have comforted us in the time since your loss, pointing out that your passing is the end of an era as you were the last of the generation who lived 'over the shop' when West Street was the heart of the town.

Sons are not the same as daughters so your nieces took a very special place in your life — Annette Masterson, Marie Higgins and Marion Neary — the sister we never had — loved you as much as we did. You were so good at holding the wider family together. You kept the Colls, the Burkes, the Cunniffes and all the branches of the Cooke clan so close, remembering all their birthdays. Your sister in law Peg Coll, was your best friend to the day you died, and her children and grandchildren meant so much to you.

Finally Mam, speaking for all the family, I want to acknowledge the love and care you experienced in your final home, Oldbridge House, Moorehall Lodge, Drogheda. To Michael and Sean McCoy, Caroline Day, Annie Radheesh and all the Oldbridge House carers, thank you so much. You are the personification of true Christianity and our lives were enriched by travelling our journey with you.

GAVIN DUFFY
Gavin Duffy is publicly known as the longest serving

'Dragon' investor on RTÉ's *Dragons' Den*. He has appeared in every series of the programme since it first aired in 2009. Gavin's early career in media included presenting the first RTÉ television business programme, *Marketplace*, and broadcasting on *Morning Ireland* before founding regional radio station LMFM.

He has spent the last 25 years working in consultancy and leadership development with some of the top names in Irish business and politics.

*I never told you that I loved you.
I suppose it's not a thing Irish male friends do.
And yet the grief was so raw, so uncontrollable,
it was clear to me that I did.*

Brian O'Connell writes to Brian Carey

Dear Brian

I was in my sitting room when I got the phone call to say you were gone. I thought there was some mistake, that the caller — a mutual friend — had mixed me up with someone else. He'd gotten the number wrong maybe, or this was some elaborate hoax or prank. Good one. Ha, Ha, Ha.

I remember having to sit down on the couch to try and physically take on board the details.

You were dead, he said. He was sorry. It looked like, well, you know... There wasn't much more he could say. The coded unsaid was clear.

Seventeen years ago, Brian, both of us were blow-ins to Cork, you from Dublin me from Ennis. We shared something of an outsiders' view of our adopted city. We lived together at times, took a holiday together, shared a passion for boxing, and for Bob Dylan. We became fathers at roughly the same time.

Over the years, we developed that private wink and nod language of delight, our own shorthand, and we had corny jokes which ran for years. Sometimes we pretended that we were old prize fighters, ready at any moment to come out of retirement. "I think you've still got a little bit left in the basement," you would say, as I'd shadow box fervently, and we'd both break into laughter.

At one point Brian you got a dog, and for years after, we pretended you had actually ordered a cat. Every time I'd call around, we'd both look at the dog, this big Labrador, and tell each other the same joke. I'd say: "That really is the funniest looking kitty I've ever seen". And you'd say something like, "Well the guy in the rescue centre assured me it was a cat." Silly stuff, I know. But jokes only we got.

I knew you had depression over the years, you were quite open about it. I knew too the year before you died you had struggled during the summer months. You phoned me one time to say you weren't in a good place, you were going into the Emergency Department. But you said you were okay and you didn't need anything and I was not to worry. So I stayed at home, but kept in phone contact with you during and after the treatment.

We chatted about it a while later and I remember you saying, "I had to get help. I surprised myself how dark a place I had gotten into." But you had counselling all set up and soon after seemed to be back to your old self. You came to my 40th birthday, and as you always did, brought the guitar and played and sang. Birthdays, weddings, New Year's Eve, you were always there with your guitar. I know your songs off by heart and many of them are there on the You Tube channel you created. Of course, when I listen to them now, all I can hear is depression. Like this one for example, called Running Up That Hill.

"And you know sometimes we can admit
That all the barriers broken down
Just how hard it can get
When the walls we build are too high to climb
And you know sometimes you can escape
When all the days they're so ordinary
The wind blows hard but who can tell

When there's every which way to turn
Oh, Yeah I know
We're only running up that hill
Only to find
There's nothing there..."

Ultimately the hill proved too high for you, my friend.

In the days and weeks after you died the grief hit me in waves. Crashing violently at first, unrelenting, then getting into its own rhythm, ebbing and flowing. I could have done more. I should have done more. Why wasn't I more present? The day you died I was working very close to your house and it crossed my mind to call up to you. But I didn't. We hadn't seen each other as much in the weeks beforehand. Now I know it's because you were struggling. I wasn't alert enough to it. Suicide leaves so many questions, and part of me will always feel guilt. Always feel I could have done more, could have been a better friend to you, could have saved you. Looking back, there are things I would do differently.

Through my work as a journalist with RTÉ, I've often reported on the need to be upfront around issues to do with mental health, and yet here it was hiding in plain sight beside me and I couldn't see it or didn't want to see it.

I never told you that I loved you. I suppose it's not a thing Irish male friends do. And yet the grief was so raw, so uncontrollable, it was clear to me that I did. Previously to this the only grief I'd felt was when my grandparents had died, and although that was emotional, they had lived long lives.

You were only 46, Brian, a father to a beautiful daughter I have known since she was a toddler. It was far too soon.

In the months after you died, I wanted to talk about grief, to try make sense of this emotion we will all probably experience. After the initial days and weeks passed, I remember sitting one day in a coffee shop in Cork and thinking grief was actually quite a beautiful thing on one level. It takes you by the hand and shows you how much you really cared for someone. Could grief ever be good though, when it is prompted by such a negative?

I was fortunate to be able to make a radio programme, *Life After Loss*, which aired on RTÉ Radio 1 the Christmas after you died. In it I tried to make sense of grief, and met with people who've developed their own relationship with it. What I learned from making that programme is that everyone experiences grief differently, and that you have to form your own personal relationship with it, a relationship that allows you to both acknowledge your grief, but also to not be weighed down by it.

I've learned that as time goes on, it's not so much the big events that catch you out, the birthdays or the anniversaries or Christmas. For me grief can often be hiding in the mundane, the ordinary life events — the smell of a room, a song on the radio, the way someone catches your eye on the street. I've learned, too, never to take friendship for granted again, to be overcautious when it comes to the mental health of those around me, and to be very direct when trying to ascertain whether or not someone may be suicidal.

None of this of course will bring you back, my friend. I miss you, and I miss our friendship. I miss the shorthand of it, the decades of back references and in-jokes, the feeling of knowing that there was someone on the end of a phone that got me. I've spent a lot of time in the past year reading about grief and talking to people who have lost someone. While we're very good at doing death in Ireland, I'm not so sure we do grief very well. But as the old cliché goes, it really is good to talk, and to try to contextualise grief.

One of the quotes that struck me most in recent months was a line in a letter written by, of all people, Queen Elizabeth II, to families of missing victims shortly after 9/11. In it, she said: "Grief is the price we pay for love."

It's a hell of a price to pay, but one that is, ultimately, worth paying.

Your friend, Brian

BRIAN O'CONNELL
Brian O'Connell is an award winning RTÉ journalist and producer. He made the 2017 RTÉ Radio 1 documentary, *Life After Loss*, as a tribute to one of his closest friends — musician and songwriter Brian Carey, who took his own life. Previously, Brian's first non-fiction book, *Wasted*, examined Ireland's relationship with alcohol and was published by Gill & Macmillan.

Why should I be out of mind
Because I am out of sight?
I am but waiting for you,
For an interval, somewhere very near,
Just around the corner.

Ollie Campbell writes to Ray Gravell

Dear Grav

You are sadly missed, and it is no exaggeration to say that Llanelli, Wales and the whole rugby World has been a much less colourful place without you in it in the past decade or so.

You were a passionate and proud Welshman and a totally unique character, and the only person in the world who always called me by my first name — Seamus — pronounced with a strong Irish accent of course! In memory of you, by mutual consent as you probably know, Mari has continued this tradition since you passed away.

You were the warmest, most magical and exuberant human being imaginable. It was an honour to have played with you and against you, and a privilege and a blessing to have known you. You epitomised everything that is good in rugby and indeed everything that is good in the human spirit.

From a distance you appeared fearless, intimidating, imposing and indestructible. What made you so appealing was the fact that in reality you were so vulnerable. You had such an engaging personality you enriched the lives of everyone you came in contact with throughout your life.

We first met in St Ermin's Hotel in London on the eve of our departure to South Africa with Bill Beaumont's Lions in 1980. You pulled me aside to say how delighted you were to meet me. I was extremely flattered by this, but then somewhat confused when you said you felt we could be soul mates on tour, as you had heard that I was reserved, quiet and even shy — just as you were yourself!!

On that tour we played Orange Free State in Bloemfontein. In the very first play of the game you made a tackle on your opposite number, De Wet Ras, that was so late it was almost posthumous. Asked to comment on this on TV afterwards, you explained that since you were a young boy you had always been told how important it was to get your first tackle in early — even if it's late!

It was on that tour that I first witnessed your pre-match dressing room routine. You alternately cried with emotion, as you listened and sang along with your favourite Welsh ballad singer Dafydd Iwan on your Walkman, and vomited with nerves in the toilet.

Apart from being a player and a commentator on rugby you were a great ambassador for the game. But due to your broadcasting and acting career — and your personality — your influence went way beyond rugby. I was always particularly intrigued that you lived on Heol Ray Gravell — Ray Gravell Road — where Mari lives to this day. How many people live on a road named after them?!

After you passed away on Oct 31st 2007, 35 years to the day since you played for Lllanelli and famously beat the All Blacks 9 to 3 — probably the proudest day of your life — in an extraordinary outpouring of emotion over 10,000 people turned up at Stradey Park to pay their last respects. Not a bad turnout for such a reserved, quiet and shy man!

Ten years later on Oct 31st 2017 at a dinner in your honour it was announced that The Ray Gravell Foundation has now raised over 1 million pounds for the local community, so your influence lives on.

In addition to this there is now a one man play called "Grav" which has been so successful in Wales in the past two years it is making its debut on Broadway on St Patrick's weekend this year. It is set in the dressing room in Stradey Park, a place you graced so many times. What a singular tribute this is to the impact you made in your 56 years. How many people have a play named after them?!

Exactly ten years ago this year I tragically lost my youngest brother Michael. Just like you he was a "social butterfly" and just like you his legacy is in his laugh and his smile. You would have loved him.

At his funeral his wife Ciara asked me to read a Reflection called *Death Is Nothing At All*.

I am going to recall that Reflection here, as I feel the words and the sentiment could so easily be reassuring ones from you to Mari, Gwenan, Manon, all your relations and the many hundreds of friends who have missed you so much since you left this mortal World in 2007.

Death is nothing at all,
It does not count.
I have only slipped away into the room next door.
Everything remains as it was.
The old life that we lived together so fondly together
Is untouched, unchanged.
Whatever we were to each other that we still are.

Call me by the old familiar name.
Speak of me in the way which you always used.
Put no sorrow in your tone.
Laugh as we always laughed at the

Little jokes that we shared together.
Play, smile, think of me, pray for me.
Let my name be ever the household
Word that it always was.
Let it be spoken without effort.

Life means all that is ever meant.
It is the same as it ever was.
There is unbroken continuity.
Why should I be out of mind
Because I am out of sight?
I am but waiting for you,
For an interval, somewhere very near,
Just around the corner.
All is well. Nothing is hurt, nothing is lost.
One brief moment and all will be as it was before.
How we shall laugh at the trouble of parting when we
meet again.

Grav, it is said that to be forgotten is to die twice, but
you will never be forgotten. And on behalf of Mari and the
girls and everyone you met in your life I will conclude with
the words of St John Chrysostom, former Archbishop of
Constantinople, who once said "those whom we have loved
and lost are no longer where they were before. They are
now wherever we are".

Rest in Peace — until we meet again.
Yours sincerely,
Ollie

OLLIE CAMPELL

Ollie Campbell is an Irish rugby legend, described as the architect-in-chief of Ireland's 1982 Triple Crown victory, the first since 1949. He was the leading scorer in that year's Five Nations Championship, and again the following year giving Ireland a joint championship along with France. In all he was capped 22 times for Ireland, and also capped seven times for the British and Irish Lions. His so called 'rivalry' with Tony Ward regularly made headlines, starting in 1979 when *The Irish Press* newspaper put the headline WARD OUT, CAMPBELL IN above a story about Pope John Paul 11 visiting Ireland.

> *I resolved there and then that while you might be dead to the rest of the world, you would still live in my head and heart every day.*

PJ Cunningham writes to Mary Jo Cunningham

Dear Mam

It's over 18,000 days now since you slipped quietly into the hot August night of 1968.

I wasn't there as they gathered around you to recite the rosary as the clock chimed midnight. As a 12-year-old I had been sent to bed but was roused by my cousin with the words "your Mammy's dead."

By the time I ran down to the front room and pushed through the crowd of neighbours and relatives gathered in sad reverence there, your eyes were indeed closed under your glasses and your body was stilled — no longer gasping rhythmically up and down for breath as had been the case for all of the previous week.

You had two last wishes which you delivered ceremoniously from your propped up state in the "little room" bed the previous Saturday to the three of us. You wanted Daddy, my brother and I to always look out for one another because you said you had not long left. You also asked that we fill the room with the aroma of rosemary and lavender — it would rid the place of the scent of your death, you said.

With the rosary down to the Hail Holy Queen, I stood in front of your face waiting for a breath to return. Seeing me, family put sympathetic arms around my shoulders, gently whispering that you had gone to a better place.

I resolved there and then that while you might be dead to the rest of the world, you would still live in my head and heart every day. I had no intention of walking down through the decades of my life with you rapidly fading as an image backwards in my mind like something long passed in a rearview mirror.

The day of your funeral was the first gut-bursting sad occasion I encountered; we stood side by side watching family, friends and neighbours take turn at shovelling earth onto your coffin.

You were a great woman for quotations and you taught me about the beauty of poetry and encouraged me to find my own favourites. As you were dying, I turned to Emily Dickinson, who had a fascination about this life and the next. Right now as indeed at that moment of utter change in my life, her words were sustaining.

"Unable are the loved to die. For love is immortality," said the poet. Behind my tears I repeated those words so, to quote Dylan Thomas, death would have no dominion over me at the graveside.

Another wise man Robert Frost was slightly more prosaic when he proclaimed that he could explain everything he'd learned about life in three words — "it goes on."

I would find how true that statement was and that waking up every morning hoping your death had been a dream, was really a young boy's folly and not real life. Yet for all the relentless movement of the clock, there have been occasions when time has stood still for me and you have been brought back to life.

Like the time in 1982 when I met an Irish family from my home town in the Bronx while I was over to play football for Offaly in New York. She was part of my friend's family and when we sat down for dinner, she asked me who my parents were.

"Frank and Mary Jo Cunningham from the Green," I answered, hoping that she had fond memories of them both.

Instead she shook her head.

As her husband stood up to put food on her plate, he gestured with a manic twirling of his finger to his own head behind her back.

"My wife has dementia," he whispered as he passed the vegetable bowl down to me.

I nodded in understanding.

My friend and his uncle began talking about families and people from our little town.

Half way through the meal, the lady with 'dementia' interrupted. "I only knew one Mary Jo. It was Mary Jo Dillon. She worked in the Post Office and helped me with my money as I was preparing to come to America. She told me that she was sad I was leaving the town and said she hoped I'd come back one day. Do you know her?"

I was dumbstruck. My eyes welled up.

"She was my mother," I said.

That moment of realisation that my mother's memory burnt fondly in the heart of a woman suffering from dementia often sustains me when I try to put flesh back on memories over half a century old.

Sometimes too there are milestones — like a decade ago when I surpassed your 52 years and 301 days on earth. It made me realise how short a time you were dealt.

Since then I've found daily comfort without recourse to poets' words or need to head-butt my own reality.

Every day since I passed your time on earth I've managed to walk again in your presence. Picking a stick of rosemary or lavender growing side by side in a spot I visit daily to give our dog her constitutional gives me the scent — not of your death, but of your life.

PJ CUNNINGHAM

PJ Cunningham is an editor, publisher and journalist who is also the author of the trilogy, *The Lie of the Land*, *A Fly Never Lit* and *The Long Acre*, which was shortlisted for Irish Book Of The Year in 2014.

He also wrote *A.N. Other* in 2001 and has written and edited *Around The Farm Gate* and co-edited *Then There Was Light*, a book about the rural electrification of Ireland, and *From The Candy Store To The Galtymore*, an anthology of stories from the golden age of the Irish showband era that stretched from the 1950s to the 1970s.

A native of Clara, Co Offaly, PJ now lives in Bray, Co Wicklow with his wife Rosemary and family of five.

Finbar Furey writes to Donna

Donna

A piece of broken heart
Weeps within my breast
Golden hair, laughing eyes
Lovely girl at rest.
I can see the dimples when she smiled
Her warm and gentle way
I close my eyes to sleep at night
I hear her sad voice say –
Mind my babes, brother dear
Take them to your side
Tell them I will love them
Until the end of time.

© Finbar Furey 1988
For a dear friend I still see.

FINBAR FUREY
Finbar Furey is a musician, singer, songwriter and poet.
　　With the band, The Fureys, he released the best selling records *When You Were Sweet Sixteen*, *The Green Fields of France*, *Leaving Nancy*, *Red Rose Café*, *The Lonesome Boatman* and many more. They were the first Irish folk group to play on *Top of The Pops*. He wrote this poem for a dear friend who died too young.

About Our Lady's Hospice

SINCE its establishment in 1879 by the Congregation of the Religious Sisters of Charity, Our Lady's Hospice & Care Services has taken a holistic approach to end-of-life care, looking to the individual needs of patients and their families. Almost 140 years later that precious charitable ethos remains unaltered.

Today, it meets patient needs from rehabilitation to end-of-life care on its two sites, Harold's Cross and Blackrock, and in homes across south Dublin and north Wicklow.

Over 600 staff, 330 volunteers and one therapy dog provide excellent loving care on-site in Harold's Cross and Blackrock Hospice. In addition, a 25-strong specialist community palliative care team provide professional care in homes across south Dublin and north Wicklow, making over 10,700 visits annually.

Staff and volunteers focus on the person and not the condition understanding that each person has unique needs. Patients are treated like family and the hospice as their home.

Specialist palliative care comprising physical, psychological, social and spiritual support is provided in Harold's Cross and Blackrock. This holistic approach includes families and caregivers and provides a range of bereavement supports.

The 22-acre Harold's Cross campus is also home to two other services: Care of the Older Person and the Rheumatic and Musculoskeletal Disease Unit.

The Care of the Older Person Unit is made up of Anna Gaynor House and the Community Reablement Unit (CRU). The former is a long-stay facility with gerontological expertise, which also supports younger residents with neurological conditions. CRU is designed to support those aged over 65 who want to remain living independently in their own homes, using programmes designed to suit each individual.

The Rheumatic and Musculoskeletal Disease Unit supports those living with arthritis, rheumatic disease, fibromyalgia and other bone and muscle diseases. Two to three week programmes are devised to improve or maintain the quality of life of patients.

Our Lady's Hospice & Care Services recently completed its most significant project to date, a €15m redevelopment of its 36 single-bed specialist palliative care unit in Harold's Cross to meet the increased demand and ensure the best quality facility for patients and their families.

About the Editor

Without You — Living With Loss has been devised, compiled and edited by Orlaith Carmody. It is her second book. Her first title, *Perform As A Leader*, also by Ballpoint Press, was published in 2015.

Orlaith is the Managing Director of Gavin Duffy and Associates, which specialises in communications training and leadership development. As a keynote speaker, conference chair and seminar leader, Orlaith has addressed Ireland's most influential business people, networks and political groups. She has also presented at conferences in the USA, UAE, Canada and throughout Europe.

Following a career as a broadcast journalist with RTÉ, Orlaith became an entrepreneur, and is a director of a number of companies. She served on the board of RTÉ from 2010 to 2015, HRM Recruit from 2011 to 2016, and is currently the Chairperson of HCCI — Home and Community Care Ireland. She is a founder member of the Irish Chapter of EO, the Entrepreneurs' Organisation, and was President 2014/15. She lives on the Louth/Meath border with her husband Gavin Duffy and four children, now young adults.